Secrets of The Dark Arts Covert Persuasion:

Influence, Manipulation, and Words that Change Minds

Written by

Arthur Cannon

Table of Contents

Introduction

Welcome to and thank you for choosing **Covert Persuasion: Influence, Manipulation, and Words that Change Minds**, a book designed to enhance and support your natural ability to shape the world around you without having to suffer the malice or manipulations of others.

Every word we speak, write or post on social media influences those we interact with. This happens automatically for better or worse and in most cases haphazardly at best. This book sets out methods for recognising what causes these automatic reactions and tactics for using this newfound knowledge to your advantage. For anyone curious about the ways in which we influence others, be it conscious or unconsciously in the hopes of improving their personal communication skills. Through analysing personal communication styles and preferences, patterns can be established and specific words begin to stand out for their reliability and their effect. A lot of the hard work has been done for you, the book contains countless examples and exercises that can be put into use for immediate results and when repeated and considered over time will reveal endless findings and new information.

The idea of the covert persuasion of others has certain negative associations, however, with ethical consideration and creativity, any moral uncertainties can be overcome. If you are interested in exploring the moral implications and moral pitfalls surrounding covert persuasion, the previous book in the **Secrets of** the **Dark Arts** series **Psychological Manipulation: Analyzing People, Situations and How to Influence Others Through Covert Persuasion** goes into depth on the subject.

Life is full of struggle and problematic situations, some of us take the brunt of these realities head-on while a great many others choose to live life the way of the troglodyte (in the dark). The popular choice is to casually put off and avoid most non-critical issues, but doing so soon causes small problems to increase in size until either they grow overwhelming in sheer number or combine and evolve into much more serious problems. A truly artful approach to persuasion is one that solves the problems of others at the same time as it fulfills our own needs. However. This cannot be accomplished through crude bargaining and a 'you scratch my back and I'll scratch yours' level of thinking. Methods like these lead to feelings of resentment and underlying disgust and so we must be subtle in any approach we choose to make. If someone feels like they're being manipulated, pressured or lied to, their internal alarm bells are going to start ringing and so we need to offer a solution in such a way that these alarms are not triggered. To achieve this, we must take our time, choose our moment, and not let our own emotions cloud our ability to read other people, their intentions, emotional states, and their situation as a whole. We must speak to the underlying needs that are going unfulfilled or to the mounting pressure they are feeling and that your proposed methodology, technique or initiative will alleviate their stress or provide them with much-needed validation or phoney elite status. We can do this through the thoughtful and creative use of language, the placing of particular words, with pauses and speech patterns which when used alongside congruent body language have miraculous effects. This book aims to shed some light on the use of particular words and phrases to influence the emotions and decision-making process' of other people as well as opening your mind to deeper levels of communication. Mastering the proper use of words is an incredible, yet mostly overlooked skill and it is the aim of this book to bring to light the brilliance and effectiveness of skills like storytelling and developing charisma. Just these two skills alone have the ability to magnify your current personal influence many times over. In the name of influence and persuasion, you will learn how to create your own conversational 'Eriksonian' language patterns, use the emotions of the crowd to your advantage, persuade superiors, keep subordinates in check, and win arguments against both groups and individuals. Towards the end of the book, there is a chapter covering some of the greatest conmen of the past 200 years, their adventures, and exactly how they exploited their fantastic knowledge of human nature to become legendary folk heroes of the 19th and 20th centuries. The book finished with some last do's, don'ts

Charisma

Personal impact can be described as charisma, but charisma is difficult to measure. However, its power rises above social standing, wealth and destroys preconceived prejudices. Mysterious in nature, charisma is thought to be the gift of the chosen few and a very powerful gift at that. In reality, charisma is the ability to make an outstanding, emotionally charged and lasting impression on those we meet. Charisma, personal influence, and likeability at first seem difficult, even elusive concepts to grasp, however, all three can be summed up simply. They spring from the affects you have on the feelings of those around you. Those who have and utilise their charisma naturally influence those around them as they radiate both competence and confidence.

The previously discussed flexibility of a leader and self-awareness are the first steps to creating and enhancing more impactful interactions. These alongside the proper education and implementation of skills will boost your influence and perceived charisma many times over.

Improving our personal impact can be done in a number of ways. The most effective strategy is to focus on the individual areas needing improvement one at a time, and over time they form a solid foundation of self-knowledge, communicative and personal skills. There are numerous courses, tools, and classes available to those hoping to boost their charisma, however, in this book, I will only be discussing ideas and methods that:

- Call for no financial investment
- Are simple to understand
- Can be tried and tested immediately

Developing Charisma

Over time we all develop bad habits that only serve to hold us back. Many of these habits go unnoticed or unchecked as we carry many of them through childhood and into our adult lives. Our friends and family chalk them up to personality quirks and so never mention them to us. These 'quirks' usually hinder our personal impact rather than help it and so we must yet again be vigilant of our own behaviours and how they are interpreted by others. Further to moderating our own actions, we can also improve our perceived charisma through practice and analysis.

No matter what point we are at in our lives one of the most influential and useful tools available to us is our charisma. Getting along with people and telling a few jokes is one thing but if we need our charisma to have a lasting impact and be powerful enough to influence individuals or command an entire audience, we must develop our charisma beyond likeability with the aim of inspiring loyalty and devotion in our audience.

There are solid methods that can be used to enhance our charisma, many of these are communicated non-verbal behaviours that can be learned and practiced until they become internalised and using them becomes second nature. Here are some of the most useful methods and techniques that individually will increase your charisma effect, but when combined and used effectively will draw others to you and create countless opportunities to persuade and influence others.

Make yourself comfortable. Whether we are walking, standing, sitting, or leaning we must do so in a comfortable way. If we set ourselves down uncomfortably and try to just put up with the uncomfortableness this will not be missed by those around us. Our posture will look 'off' and we will fidget which may cause others to assume we are displaying deceptive traits. Not properly clearing our throats before speaking might cause it to sound scratchy which people will assume means that we lack confidence in what we are saying.

- In addition to the above, wear clothes that fit, proper shoes, and learn how to properly tie a tie. You will look and feel better and as a result, you will be more comfortable and confident.
- Maintain eye contact-just not too much. It has been scientifically proven that when people look us directly in the eyes during our interactions are seen as attractive and trustworthy. Eye contact is a subtle skill that appeals to everyone,

improves intimacy and sincerity and enhances the quality of all of our interactions.

- Place your devices on silent and keep it in your pocket or bag. Looking at your phone during a conversation or negotiation is common a problem as ever there one. Indulging in phone/screen time whilst in the presence of other stirs negative feelings of rejection. We want our audience to feel they have our full attention, which they deserve and should receive, especially if we are speaking to them one to one. Using your mobile device in social situations is not just viewed as rude, it is rude. No matter how many others are doing it we should always refrain from using our phones in social situations whenever possible.

- Let people know that you are listening to them and that you understanding them by gently nodding from time to time and asking questions to further clarify their standpoint. Ask them if you understand them clearly enough and summarise a few of their key points.

- Allow the other person to completely finish their point before formulating your response. Take your time in giving your reply or rebuttal, this shows that you are considering what they have said and also allows you time to go over your options before answering.

- Take a little time to study the enigmatic leaders and communicators of the past. Research famous examples that are similar to your current situation and learn from them.

Motivating Factors

As human beings, we all share a great many motivating factors in common. The need for food, shelter, warmth, protection, a semblance of a social life, all these things and more we share in commonality worth every other human being on the planet. There are, however, three motivating factors that come into play more often than any other and these are the desire for money, power/influence, and of course, sex.

- Financial rewards, bribes, backhand deals, and cash equivalents have been popular motivators and incentives since the creation of money. Before this time these types of rewards would have been in the form of goods and services (cash equivalents). Money, to most of us, represents true freedom and so it is arresting in its persuasiveness and coercive in nature. It is the most commonly used exploitative power on the planet and has been effectively used to influence kings and peasants alike since the beginning, none of us are safe. Offering cash money as an incentive is too crude and costly, our hard-won assets have better uses than giving them away. So, instead try using the threat of potential financial losses as an influencer. Explain how the other sides views and actions will lead to financial loss in the very near future and how your methods will at worst keep the wolf away from the door. Financial freedom can be translated as personal security, this is interesting because it gives us options beyond just throwing cash around. If we can provide a sense of improved personal security, our audience is almost guaranteed to succumb and convert to our way of thinking.

- Empowerment through increased involvement helps us all. Many of us (myself included) have the problem of wanting to everything ourselves and we struggle to delegate meaningful tasks to others. However, sharing responsibility for a project or task with one or more people is actually essential to lasting and sustainable success. Here is a technique that will allow you to convert complainers and those with low moral before they infect the rest of the team with their negativity. Try giving extra responsibility to someone who is less than enthusiastic about the project will significantly improve their moral. They will feel superior to other team members which will invariably suit their personality type and also give them something to focus their energy on, and once they earnestly commit their energy, they always work hard because their own ego will by now be invested in the success of the project.

- You may be wondering exactly what is meant by the desire for sex, for our purposes sex doesn't need to be the act itself. Human interaction, acknowledgement the feeling of being accepted by others is as irresistible to us as they are intoxicating. Receiving admiration and finding an affinity with someone of the opposite sex might be viewed as trivial interactions, however trivial they may be, we all crave the acceptance and closeness to others these interactions bring. Being empathetic, considerate and giving those we communicate with our full attention will create worthwhile connections and mutual understanding that will provide those we interact with feelings of security, relaxation, and trust while in your presence.

Beyond money, power, and sex the next motivator in line of significance is the feeling of being appreciated. Showing appreciation has an immediate and lasting effect. People remember those that show them appreciation to them and acknowledge their efforts. Sincerely showing appreciation to someone instantly disarms them, alleviates their stress levels, and allows them to feel understood. We are all instinctually drawn to those who recognise and appreciate our achievements, so do more than simply saying thanks, look someone in the eye, pick an aspect of their character or actions and thank them for their help in this regard, doing this will make you come across as more genuine. Shake their hand if appropriate and congratulate them whenever possible.

Try asking someone to do you a small favour, for instance, ask them to bring you a glass of water, show them appreciation in earnest and strike up a conversation about them. Ask them a few open-ended questions, allow them to speak and when the time is right, make your true request and make them aware that you will greatly appreciate their help. This technique hugely increases the likelihood of your request being granted.

What Does it Take to Convince You?

In order to convince, convert, influence or persuade we must first make things interesting. An audience whose interest is lacking will rapidly lose attention and get bored and so we must constantly cater to and refer back to the individual and focus on their needs whatever they may be. We are interested in what applies to us either by means of perceived danger, increased security, greater wealth, or social acceptance and connecting an idea or initiative to one or more of these primary factors will add a great deal of weight to your position. The language models, tactics and hacks mentioned in the book will help you to speak and write in a way that naturally captivates the mind, however, to be fully effective the deeper message must be one that charms and fascinates the listener.

Presentation

The way in which we make our approach sets the tone for the whole interaction and greatly effects the personal experience of all involved. When we appear knowledgeable, competent and trustworthy from the outset, our persuasive magic is already in action paving the way for us before we speak a word. The audience instantly makes assumptions about us and our message and so we must draw their attention to positive factors that we outwardly display then grab their attention by beginning with what the audience will consider the most interesting and important. Providing a sense of

'I'm here to help' or "I came to you because you're helpful" adds a human feel from the offset and

Build A Coalition

Generally speaking, it is easier for a group to convince a lone individual than it is for the lone individual to convince a group. It is for this reason that it is important that whenever possible you should add to our list of advocates; this will give you an air of authority and greatly increase your influence over all involved. When building a coalition, start by assessing all those who will either need to be involved or may be affected in some way by your initiative and assess their sphere of influence. Is there anyone who needs to be pacified from the outset? Is there anyone who you absolutely need on your side? Does anyone have access to the resources we need? And who, if anyone can strengthen our political power base? Start with these individuals and then look to those who are popular or possess a large following and in time the rest of the crowd will surely follow, with little need of convincing.

Be Inclusive

Invite others to express their opinions and get creative with things like process and other non-consequential factors. Give dissenters phony titles that will allow them to feel superior to the crowd and they will soon be loyal supporters of your cause. By sticking to the overall aim while encouraging the input of others you will engage them creatively which will leave them feeling emotionally invested in your cause. Target the loners in the group ask for their advice and mirror their thinking, by asking for opinions and support from the outsider you gain a loyal and resourceful advocate. Given the opportunity, everyone will prove themselves to be useful, we all have untapped resources within us and all it takes is for someone with understanding to properly direct us.

Symbolism

The effectiveness of symbols in non-verbal communication and persuasion has been exploited time and again throughout history for two reasons above all others. Through the use of symbolism, we are able to associate either ourselves or our cause with something much greater than ourselves, something that carries specific emotional attachments and truths no one can deny. This was one of the many tactics employed by the greatest of all French monarchs 'The Sun King' Louis XIV (1638-1715). Furthermore, doing so completely bypasses any cognitive resistance as no argument is being made but an effect is felt, a seed is sown. A symbol can be anything from shapes (pyramids), objects (The Grail), animals (lion), colours (gold), or anything else that suits your overall goal and also increases your influence. The goal itself can be symbolic in origin much in the same way a university degree is the goal of all attending students. The aim is unconscious acceptance by others of the association between yourself or your goal and your chosen symbol. This can be achieved in a number of ways including:

- Carefully placed images of the symbol.
- Repeatedly referencing the symbol and its similarities with the current mood or desired change.
- Motifs/Logos/Mascots.
- Clothing, music and other props.

We've all had experiences with symbolism, in modern society with are constantly bombarded with symbols designed to inspire everything from religious devotion, what burger we should eat, where we should shop and what we should buy, and even how we choose our relationships. However, the use of symbolism can sometimes be tricky to grasp so here are a few examples of the power of symbolism in action:

- The Prime Minister will give a speech in front of their countries flag in order to inspire feelings of patriotism.
- Film characters with names that are associated with lightning in some way indicate that they are in some way fast.

- During an advertisement for cologne, an actor flashes an expensive watch and gets into his top of the line sports car to signify the success that is associated with that particular brand of aftershave.
- Advertisements for holidays will invariably show the typical 2.4 children family enjoying time together to associate their brand with family values.

Filling the Gaps

There are two main ways in which to fill in gaps and unanswered questions within an approach, pitch, or general interaction. We can take existing information that has holes in it and fill those gaps ourselves with what the finer details mean to our cause and the listener. This is a useful method that gives us a lot of control, however, once we have filled the gaps and everyone is clear on the information, we will have undoubtedly backed ourselves into some sort of corner by making promises we may not be able to keep, or taking on a later obligation. This method may be effective but it pales in comparison when compared to allowing the audience to fill in blanks with their own creativity. Allude to riches and glory and their creative process will do the rest. Provide a core value or goal to your cause that signifies virtue of some kind and pepper the way with possibilities and pride. This will allow each individual to add their own meaning by mixing it with their own internal ideas and ideals of what these possibilities could mean to them and their personal goals. This method not only fully engages and captivates the listener, it causes them to become emotionally invested in your ideas and perhaps the best part is that you don't have to make any solid promises, your back is covered, your conscience clear. Any distortion between the end results and what the listener expected can be shown to have been due to their own creativity when filling in the blanks.

Make Use of Credible Sources

Quoting a credible source can inspire the same emotional patterns as the proper use of symbolism. It is a method that bypasses the knee-jerk cognitive resistance of direct statements and requests with the added bonus that using a familiar source lowers any feelings of fear. This familiarity adds a level of comfort to proceedings. If it is possible to do so, referring to a past example with positive connotations will have a similar effect and add a feeling of safety to your newly proposed initiative. Choose past examples to provide answers to as many anticipated questions as possible. In this way you can confront and subsequently dismiss the more dangerous objections before they are voiced, effectively cutting the audience off from any opposing points of view in a most respectful and (seemingly) passive way.

The use of sources also limits the amount of blame that can be placed at our feet should everything not turn out exactly as others may have expected. Employing examples and quotes as Trojan horses to both conceal and further our intentions can be played off as an effort to provide reliable data from which everyone is able to make their own fully informed decision, when in reality we are dealing the cards and the deck we are using is heavily stacked in our favour.

Closing

Each individual's decision-making process will vary, however, there are certain things that we can do, feelings we can provoke, and situations we can stage that will help give those who are sitting on the fence that extra push needed to convert them and/or close the deal. Even if we have maxed out our persuasive strategies and our audience seems convinced, we should still make sure that we have sealed the deal and allied any internal concerns that they may have. We should consider all possible reactions and consequences prior to attempting to change someone's mind and we should do this on an individual basis because in most case resistance will be due to someone's fears, preconceptions, and past personal experiences and have little if anything to do with the finer details of your proposed ideas. Once we have listened, analysed, debunked, and countered all reasonable objections we can add further weight to our initiatives by summarising the positive consequences of our proposed initiatives and cast them against the next best idea, however, be sure to make it absolutely clear that your proposed actions will provide everything that the competition will and a whole lot more.

Another powerful method for securing the support of others is to add a sense of urgency to the decision-making process. Ensure this sense of urgency focuses wholly on the listener as any urgency sensed coming from the speaker will be viewed as weakness or worse, deception. Throw in a deadline, if there isn't a reason for the deadline, make one up. Adding a last-minute incentive can be framed as a personal touch, a gift even, that shows why your idea or service is the best option available. Done correctly, the individual you are attempting to convert will feel like you like them and will not want to let you down and therefore risk spoiling the image of them that they believe you hold. This, plus the law or reciprocation will in most cases be enough to cement our position and convince our audience as to our way of thinking.

Mastering Emotions

The first and most important thing to understand is that the only reason anyone does anything is to change the way they feel a situation, another person, or themselves.

Decades of research conducted by psychologists, psychiatrists, and self-help gurus the world over tells us that there are a handful of primary factors that contribute to our overall emotional state and how we define, experience and react to each moment as it arrives. Such aspects are often interconnected and create emotional loops that regularly repeat themselves when we face excitement, difficult situations, and times of happiness or stress. Over a lifetime these loops repeat and overlap thousands of times until, in the end, they act as an autopilot programme and the poor affected individual becomes more and more predictable in behaviour and easier to manipulate and control by all who wish to try.

Fortunately for us, these determining factors exist within the realm of our control, but before we can steer and guide them, we must be able to recognise them. Following chapters will go into more depth on recognising and guiding the emotional states of others but at this point the focus of attention is our own emotions, recognising our personal triggers and self-control. There will be times when we are more or less emotional, for instance, if we happened to miss lunch, or have a migraine we may be prone to frustration and anger, yet whatever the internal conflict we must remain composed and unaffected. Mastery over one's emotions is one of the most powerful skills at our disposal and one that has a positive effect on all aspects of life. It is not easy; you must stay constantly vigilant of your own tendencies and reactions in order to temper and redirect them toward appropriate and desired outcomes. Primarily we must learn to understand ourselves.

What Am I Feeling?

Take comfort in the fact that your emotions are there to serve a purpose, they are trying to tell you something, they may at times be incorrect or act on a false premise, unproductive pettiness, or even revenge, yet what really matters is that they are there to help. The crucial part is not how we are feeling, but how we interpret and use this information to best serve our current agenda. Our levels of motivation or lack of, and complete inaction are almost always caused by our current emotional state and quality of thinking. Often times our emotions are kick started by triggers that elicit specific emotional states, however, by learning to recognising these triggers they quickly become ridiculous to us, as does our previous reaction to them, at which point we have officially made significant progress. These new revelations will impact your actions, improving them and magnifying your success many times over.

Emotions are not exclusive to themselves; they are interconnected and span an entire emotional spectrum, some connections are clear such as sadness and anger (anger is said to be the bodyguard of sadness) and love and excitement, yet even some of the lesser known and rarely spoken of connections have proved the most useful to marketers, religious sects, and spoilt children the world over. The link between guilt and generosity creates a magical effect and a particularly strong call to action. The beauty of using the link between guilt and generosity as a persuading factor is that even if the call is initially ignored it will grow more powerful over time. Do not let the target forget their guilt, it is an unbearable emotion which people will do anything to dispel and by subtly keeping it in the forefront the weight of it will soon leave the target no option but to do what it takes to rid themselves of it by converting wholeheartedly to our way of thinking. Emotions move people, but more on that later.

Whenever we feel unfavourable emotions rearing their head it is difficult to deal with them logically, however, what we can do is adapt and change the emotion to a more helpful one in next to no time. We can do this in three main ways:

Our **body language** and physiology play a major role in determining our emotional and mental state. It is well known that power poses give our confident an almost instant boost much in the same way as sitting slouched staring at the floor will soon leave you feeling melancholy and even depressed. Assuming the proper posture not only brings about change within us but affects the way in which we are viewed by others, making body language and controlled posturing essential tools in both self-development and persuading others. Avoid slouching, only lean where it is necessary and natural to do so, keep your head up, distribute your body weight evenly, and relax the shoulders. Tense or hunched shoulders are a clear sign of low-level stress, even if in the most part you are unaware of it, regularly take notice of your shoulders and if they are at all lifter or tense, take a few deep breaths and as you exhale, allow the shoulder to relax and lower to a resting position.

Sitting back in a chair and placing your hands behind your head is one of the best postures for lifting the mood. Within seconds of taking on the position you will begin to feel a shift in perspective as feelings of confidence and even superiority stir within, positively effecting your thought pattern and dispelling feelings of doubt and inferiority. Standing up straight has a similar effect as the feeling of being literally at our tallest brings on feelings of empowerment and competence. The beautifully simple and fast acting method of adopting specific postures to enhance and adapt emotional states can be used anywhere, anytime, and is ideal for situations where we find ourselves waiting, for example, a delayed meeting, job interview, or date.

For more on analysing and effecting others with body language see the previous release in the **Secrets of The Dark Arts** series **Psychological Manipulation: Analyzing People, Situations and How to Influence Others Through Covert Persuasion**, this book goes into great depth on the subject of body language, analysing that of other people as well as our own.

Equally important is our **internal verbal communication**. The words we choose as well as the patterns, speed, pitch, and tone of our speed all contribute to the way we feel. By learning to properly control the way we speak (something we will cover later) we can massively boost our influence over not only our own moods but also the moods of those around us. Words carry connections and associations transcending the literal meaning of the word itself. Be kind when speaking to yourself, do not unnecessarily berate yourself over minor mishaps and past transgressions. Many of us are nothing short of abusive when we speak to ourselves and this type of self-communication is devastating to both confidence and productivity. Never make excuses for yourself but be fair and measured in your self-criticisms, make high demands of yourself but ensure your goals are achievable for mortals, and over time confidence will grow and acceptance of self will follow.

Focus and quality of attention have a huge effect on mood and productivity. In other words, when we focus on happy and positive things, we feel happy and positive, and when we focus on unhappy or negative things, we feel unhappy and negative. We feel what we focus on and therefore any desired mood should be available to us at any time we wish. With a little self-control, practice and perhaps even the aid of NLP (Neuro-Linguistic Programming) general mood control is easily attainable through choice of focus and power of will.

Thought Patterns, Emotions, and Their Effect on 'Presence'

The way you feel and the way you act are both determined by the way in which you think. This is common knowledge, yet unfortunately, it is overlooked by the masses. Once we internalise this simple idea, we are instantly led towards the notion of identifying the 'true' thoughts and feelings of others by reverse engineering their actions and emotional outbursts. We actually do this naturally, all the time, but as with many of the skills that have evolved alongside the human race, nowadays it is regularly ignored. In reality, our baseline emotions and the basic theme of the thoughts attached are exceedingly simple to categorise. The three main ways in which we think are as follows:

- Past
- Present
- Future

When we overthink events from the past or overindulge in imagining a terrible future it leaves us feeling uncomfortable. The past must be analysed, that much is assuredly true, however, when we delve too deep for too long it affects the way we act in the present and the effect is rarely positive.

Planning is essential, but obsessing over events that are unlikely to happen is not. The past should be viewed as a series of signposts, guiding us as to what we should do next in the quest of embittering ourselves and in the achieving of our objectives. It should alert us to the many pitfalls to avoid as well as highlighting proven roads to success. Looking into our future can (in moderation) be very useful. For example, if we look imagine a future in which we have succeeded, we then have the opportunity to reverse engineer our own imagined success. How did we get there? What steps did we take and when? Unfortunately, most thoughts of the future are not particularly useful. A common mistake is to go over the same up-coming problem over and over again, this creates worry and stress. A much more productive thing to do is to consider the future problem, decide on either a preventative solution or a way in which to deal with the issue once it arises. Many of us consider ways in which to deal with a future situation, come up with an ideal solution and then continue to obsess over the problem until they work themselves into a mild frenzy, at which point the original plan to overcome the problem is forgotten or not acted upon altogether.

The most productive thoughts are those related to the present. When thinking and acting in the present, the quality of our actions and our perceived presence or charismatic impact is magnified many times over. The transformative energy referred to here as presence is a much sought-after characteristic closely related to charisma. Social standing, influence, credibility, and attractiveness are primarily judged on the quality and power of our presence, making it a major influencer when it comes to first impressions. Being fully invested in the present moment adds greater depth to our presence, but what exactly do we mean by presence?

Throughout the day our thinking strategies, perspectives, and orientation changes, on a moment by moment basis. These mental shifts can be 'triggered' by almost anything at any time. To be fully present we must be vigilant of these variations and shepherd our thoughts away from past annoyances and future problems and focus primarily on what we are doing in the present. Throughout our lives, we pick up harmful habits that only serve to limit our perceived presence, such as boastful attitudes, bad time-keeping, selfish tendencies, the worst of all being unreliability. Pay close attention to your negative personality traits and obviate them as soon as they arise. Our first stirrings of emotion are usually the most effective indicators of the level and quality of our thoughts. If you are feeling nervous, there's a good chance you're thinking about the future, if you're feeling angry you will be going over old ground, remembering long past grievances.

Everything you learn from monitoring yourself can and should be applied to others in order to understand their underlying thought processes and problems. This information provides the skilful persuader with vital insights into personal weak points which can then be directly focussed on by specific strategies tailored to particular emotional states. There will be more on the nuances of persuasion in later chapters, for now, we need only be able to spot and identify the thought processes in others as indicated by their emotional state.

The below examples will give you a better idea of how thoughts relate to a person's current emotional state, however, as always remember that context will play a definitive role in any accurate analysis.

- **Anger** is caused by an immediate reaction to outside situational influences or by spending too much time thinking about the past. Anger is accompanied by rash, emotion-based thinking, and extremely limited decision making and communication skills. It is worth noting that anger is often a sign of (reaction to) an exposed weakness that cannot be overlooked, hidden or easily dealt with.
- **Sadness** too indicates we are thinking about the past (anger, with good reason, is regularly known as the bodyguard of sadness).
- **Fear** arises when we are thinking about future events. Fear is often accompanied by hesitancy or a reluctance to act.
- **Worry** is in most cases caused by obsessing over future events, which can sometimes include thoughts of the past (if certain situational conditions are repeated or replicated in some way). As with fear, worry also causes individuals to hesitate, to a fault.
- **Happy/calm** and the feeling of time 'flying' is a clear indication that you are present in the moment.

In summary, if we wish to be in the present moment our thinking must be focussed on the present and not in the past or future. Once we are fully present, we are able to focus on and improve the overall impact of our influence via 'presence' as perceived by others, which can be increased by:

- Taking an extra moment to make meaningful eye contact with each and every person present when entering a room, accompanied by a warm smile and an enthusiastic greeting.

- Letting others speak first, don't be in a rush to speak. A moments silence will allow all parties to adjust to your presence. If your audience is restless allow them to settle before you begin. If they are augmentative allow them to have their say and as they do let them know that they are being listened too and understood. You do not have to agree or comply with anything they are saying, just give them enough time to burn off the excess adrenalin.

- Become present before interacting with others. Do this by first closing your eyes, and taking a deep breath, hold it for five seconds. Notice how the cool air feels as it hits your face. Pay attention to the warmth of the sun on your skin, focus your attention on different body parts, left arm, left leg, right leg and finally right arm. This will return your attention to the present.

- Those with presence radiate energy, but where does this energy come from? It comes from being switched on to the moment, from controlling and directing our thought and energies with an air of certainty. This massively magnifies and intensifies our overall energy. Within all of us are two primary energetic forces which we can harness to increase our actual and perceived energy levels. Firstly, we draw energy from our physical selves, the alertness, and readiness of the entire body, which is largely dependent on our exercise and diet and self-control. This type of energy can evaporate into nothing in the face of nervousness and self-doubt. We also draw energy from our individual personalities, our moral, ethics, personal expectations of ourselves and willpower play a huge role here as does personal experience.

- Be congruent. When our actions are congruent with our values and emotions our accomplishments are exponentially energised and as a result of our successes, we are viewed by others as high functioning, credible individuals. The key to remember here is that, if ever we find ourselves lacking in motivation, we must first realign our values so they are in sync with completing the task at hand. In the rare instances where even our enhanced flexibility cannot align our values with the given task, the task itself must be redefined or rejected.

A common way of manipulating someone is to take their thoughts away from the present moment by either propelling them into the future or taking them back to either fond or unpleasant memories depending on which better fits your final objective. This method is extensively used in advertising and political campaigning, the gravy that claims to take your taste buds back to your childhood and mum's Sunday roast dinner, the credit agreement that offers low interest and affordable monthly payments, and especially the life insurance adds that plainly ask you to imagine what life would be like for your family if the worst should happen to you, are all advertisements designed to take you away from the present moment and your inherent critical thinking skills and replace them with either feelings of nostalgia, getting what you want now, and of being able to properly care for your family. In reality, without these powerful emotional motivators, the products or services themselves have little or nothing to do with the emotional ties they're hoping we will literally 'buy into'. And even less to differentiate them from the competition. For this reason, they must communicate directly to the emotional mind of their prospective client base. Some of the most targeted areas include:

- Bragging rights
- Elitist lifestyle/Implied superiority
- Nostalgia
- Fear of loss
- Belonging to a group
- Feelings of success
- Security

A Word on Avoidance

Avoidance is one the most prevalent motivating factors in society today, running wild through social circles and business alike affecting all of us either directly or indirectly by way of the impact of the choices and actions of others. Avoidance is slightly different to calls to action like fear of loss and the fear of not being deemed at least equal to our peers which generally coerce us to behave in a particular way or curb particular tendencies and opinions in order to get what we want or to fit in. The fear that coincides with avoidance does not feel urgent; it is a deeply buried fear that infects the decision-making process resulting in the non-action that is so fatal to success. Explained away through layers of reasoning and denial we are able to avoid facing our true issues for our entire lives; however, the cost is that we never attain the true knowledge and control of self that leads to true mastery and a happy and fulfilled life. To progress, we need to focus more on these areas that our natural inclinations want to avoid. If we want to throw a little extra weight behind our line of thinking we can develop plans that fulfil our goals but in doing so also allows our 'helper' to avoid that which they secretly wish to avoid. Most of the time avoidance happens on a subconscious level that has been operating and influencing decisions for many years. The brain hides this avoidance form itself mainly through the use of repetitive dissociative language. Dissociative language in this book can be taken for any words or speech patterns that disconnect and create distance between a person and reality, as well as their true emotional state. Denial is frequently caused and supported by dissociative language (followed by dissociative behaviour) and is generally an unhelpful emotional crutch. Denying the reality before us (as previously discussed) leads to poor decisions, actions, and results and so we want to alleviate others of these troubles whilst gaining important information and strengthening our influence over them. When it comes to dealing with others, dissociative language can be very beneficial to all parties involved. Those with the ability to dissociate highly charged individuals from there emotional knee jerk reflexes can direct (and therefore predict) all manner of interactions, calmly guiding them towards more desired outcomes.

Foundations for Arguments

We must attempt to perceive and identify the premises that contributed to the conclusions of every participant in the conversation if we are to successfully navigate and negotiate our way through discussions with argumentative individuals. Ideally, we should avoid this personality type, however, in the real world it is often the more combatant and domineering individuals that rise to influential positions and so from time to time we will be forced to engage such individuals. When doing so it is important to keep your composure and not get caught up in the highly emotive ebbs and flows of the interaction. Argumentative individuals are accustomed to interactions that escalate rapidly and often steer negotiations so that emotions do escalate. To do so is a tactic that often confuses and unnerves their opponents, allowing them to demand concessions and gain the upper hand. Resist their bait, recognise provocation for what it is, a sign of your opponents' weakness and inability to put forward a convincing argument.

Placing the burden of proof upon an argumentative and emotional person will often stir the waters enough for them to do or say something that severely damages both their message and reputation, making it very unlikely that their initiative will be put into action. Requesting that someone reiterate and expand on the finer points of what they just said will cause impatience and expose any holes in their reasoning that had been glossed over with hopes, excitement, enthusiasm, and emotive language. Questioning someone in this way will frustrate them if they have not completed their research or if they are lying, or concealing relevant information. Seek out these inconsistencies, particularly ones that can be led back to their original premise, an attack made in this way leaves little room for defence. as the more someone tries to defend or backtrack the less persuasive their argument will be.

When we find the burden of proof laid at our feet it is best that it be dealt with through the use of undeniable logic, the simpler the better. If we can make our logic simple enough our dissenter will be viewed as (and feel) foolish for even voicing their opinion. When challenged, have ready prepared or 'canned' proofs and other evidence that are compelling, conclusive, and completely bereft of weakness.

Lastly, phrases like win-win and mutually beneficial instantly lower the aggression of other negotiators, they are phrases that leave the opposition nothing to argue against. Putting forward a proposed course of action for the perceived benefit of all is something that not many people will want to go against for fear that it could damage their reputation and so framing our plans as such or by associating our ideas with these ideals we have the ability to associate our ideas with higher values than that of the competition/dissenter.

Eriksonian Language

In the world of NLP (Neuro Linguistic Programming) and hypnotherapy, Eriksonian language is a well-regarded style of communication-based on the works of the world-renowned Dr. Milton Erikson (otherwise known as the father of hypnotherapy). Primarily, it uses indirect language patterns to influence individuals on many levels, and once mastered it can quickly and smoothly guide individuals or even small groups into hypnotic states of varying degrees. It is a method that has proved itself over decades and through thousands of cases and is one that yields quick and reliable results to the skilled practitioner. The keystone to creating effective Eriksonian language patterns is empathy, having the ability to place yourself in someone else's shoes and really experience a taste of how they experience and interact with the outside world provides a deluge of information that can be noted for later use. We can never truly experience the reality of another person, although we can give it a good go if we can gather and decipher the correct information. What is the correct information? How do we get it? We have a chat in the here and now, ask clear questions about the person's present processes and avoid dwelling on any past events. As we do so they will begin to leak critical clues that shine a light on issues that they themselves may not be aware of that may be painfully out of control. These areas that are vulnerable are our entrance due to the simple fact that if someone is not paying proper attention to, or controlling an issue then it is open to our control, providing we have the skill to do so. Many people will openly reveal their personal 'thumbscrews' and the emotional crosses they bear by stating the opposite, showing too much enthusiasm, or by dramatic displays like spear shaking and chest thumping. Individuals use these unnecessary exaggerations and theatrical performances to draw attention from the inadequacy, smallness, and weakness that they feel.

A trance state, hypnotically induced or otherwise can be characterised as a moment in which we experience greater than normal levels of focus. We naturally drift in and out of trance states throughout the day, the intensity of these states varies immeasurably depending on many factors. We daydream as we perform menial tasks, we can become transfixed and locked into a compelling movie or book. Sports stars get the feeling of being in the 'zone' and feeling the flow as they compete to win and lovers drift off as they gaze into each other's eyes.

Our cause, however, does not require that we run around inducing hypnotic trances in all that we meet. Influencing attitudes and behaviours with our words relies more on communicating messages to the subconscious that bypass any conscious resistance. The unconscious mind is always listening and filtering through information and can be influenced by indirect suggestions that the listener themselves are unaware of. Patience and subtilty are essential here if we are to effectively catch the attention of the subconscious. One way of achieving this is to litter our conversation with carefully placed Eriksonian language that catches the conscious off-guard and communicates the message directly to the subconscious while the conscious mind is still trying to figure out what has just been said. Using subtle language patterns that approach the audience in an indirect way as opposed to the more traditional direct communication styles we experience is many times more powerful when it comes to influencing, manipulating, and helping others who may have a reputation for being rather difficult and resistant. Traditional conversation and communication styles are direct, regularly carry an autoreactive tone, defiance and resistance are made painfully clear and the overall message is generally blunt. Here's a couple of examples to help you decode and get to grips with the accommodating style of Eriksonian language.

Direct example:

"You smoke too much, you should quit"

Eriksonian example:

"You may wish to discover alternatives to smoking if you feel ready to do so"

Direct example:

"You've said enough"/ "Shut up"

Eriksonian example:

"You might consider moving on if you feel this to be an opportune moment"

Direct example:

"You're wasting time"

Eriksonian example:

"If you take a little time, when you are ready, you might discover new methods that give you a productive boost"

Direct example:

"I wished you'd stop complaining"

Eriksonian example:

"The release from letting go is empowering, if you believe it can be done"

It is clear that the direct examples will receive more resistance than the Eriksonian examples which are comprised of language designed to provoke the subconscious with their permissive and accommodating nature. The sincerity and consideration that naturally accompanies this type of language bypasses any direct resistance, especially when accompanied by the correct peaceful and relaxed tone. It is a style that is nothing less than generous with its attention towards the emotional needs of others, respects such needs, and obliges them, all the while using them as the trojan horse for our message.

Eriksonian language is incredibly influential, however, I'm not suggesting that everyone go out and take a crash course in hypnosis. Observe those around you and notice patterns in behaviour, attitude, or processes that occur regularly and create some language patterns that can be used again and again (it's remarkable how similar we all are when it comes to the effects of Eriksonian language). This isn't very difficult, people, motivation, and situations are surprisingly similar especially in workplace/social/family environments and it is for this reason that it is possible to craft key phrases that can persuade, assist, and guide those around you.

How to Develop Your Own Persuasive Language Patterns

When making an attempt at creating Eriksonian language patterns, they must be smooth, natural, and practiced to the point of agony so that when we say them, we do so naturally with fluidity, and precisely in flow with the present conversation. They must never be forced into a conversation, bide your tide, tailor your approach, and focus on the individual and opportunities will present themselves to present your message and exact your influence. These techniques are common in hypnosis and many types of therapy; however, they are rarely used in social settings and within general conversations.

Suggestions and Permissive Words

To make suggestions either directly or through covert methods like using Eriksonian language patterns in an attempt to influence the thought patterns and behaviours of another person are the foundation of persuasion, or what is known in therapy as 'change work'. Any suggestion made under the Eriksonian method must be done using indirect language that leaves out just enough information to stimulate and inspire the listeners subconscious so that it fills in the gaps and creates new thought patterns and behaviours. When developing our own conversational language patterns, we begin by looking at indirect and permissive words that will help to soften our message. Words like could, may, maybe, might, perhaps, notice, feeling, because, are all perfect for our purpose due to their ability to make elegant statements and suggestions that feel (to the listener) a million miles away from telling or even asking someone to do something. Here are a few examples to get you started:

"You **might** wish to **examine alternatives** to drinking so much coffee **if you feel it is right** to do so?"

"I've **noticed your breathing** is a lot better, **if you're feeling more relaxed**, perhaps redirecting energies is now our best option"

"**perhaps you're aware** that you can stop drinking before you're drunk"

When we ask someone to imagine a scenario of our design, we are in fact asking them to actively connect their imagination to our ideas or goals and doing so in a way which is overwhelmingly effective. By putting someone in a position where they can imagine themselves gaining victory or reaping some sort of reward by following our lead, we 'grease the wheels' and take an important step towards action. This type of suggestion, known as 'future pacing' to therapists fully engages the listener's imagination, leaving their creativity to fill in any blanks will lead the audience to become emotionally invested in your goals and sufficiently motivated to accomplish them.

Questions

Asking people about their feelings, emotional connections and about their personal experiences, in general, will lower their resistance in a way that appears humble and respectful. This appeals to the ego on many levels. By making our approach in the form of a question we appear to give our audience options when in fact we are dealing the cards from which they must choose. If we want to move someone, we can begin doing so by asking them about their personal experience on a past project or social event, the important thing here is that the event in question must be associated with the emotion that you want to elicit in the audience. For example, asking someone about a project that you know they had success with is likely to cause them to feel confident and even bold. Depending on the individual in question this could make them more likely to agree to a new project if we can associate it with their current emotional state. By asking a question we open the listener up and we follow up with an indirect suggestion as mentioned above, if we have gained sufficient rapport, we have a very good chance of influencing the immediate decision or behaviour. Because of this phenomenon of emotionally reliving experiences whenever they are remembered we are able to set the stage for persuasion with just a few seemingly sincere questions worded in an Eriksonian style.

Metaphors and Similes

Metaphors are one of the most powerful ways of engaging the imagination of an individual or group. By adding metaphors to our language patterns, we create further depth and create a story-like feeling, a story containing hidden suggestions that bypass any reactionary critical thinking. This bypass occurs because when we are 'listening' to a story we are not fully critically engaged. No one is telling us what to do or what to believe, we are simply absorbing information. Similes are similar to metaphors however where metaphors traditionally paint a picture by drawing a comparison between two things that are not alike, similes will do so but also provide a (usually workable) example. For example:

Metaphors

- He is riding on the wave of victory
- Hope is on the horizon
- It was a lukewarm reception
- I'm sure they'll warm up to the idea

Similes

- The plan is as good as gold
- He's busy as a bee
- The presentation was like watching paint dry
- That went south faster than a rabbit gets f@*ked

Presuppose

Developing your own Eriksonain language patterns and delivering them effectively is not just a case of employing a magical list of wonder words. A great deal of the persuasion done through conversational language patterns is accomplished with the clever use of presupposition. When attempting to persuade someone whether through conversational language patterns or any other style of persuasion our approach invariably contains many assumptions and multiple layers of presupposition. By using presumptions in our language, we allow the listener to unconsciously interpret and create the meaning for themselves. This works so well because no matter how hard we may try to successfully translate the deeper experiences and feelings of our audience we can never come close to their actual real-life personal experience of the world and so by having them create the meaning themselves from their own experience, the audience will create a much more powerful connection than we ourselves would have been able to elicit with our words alone. A presupposition is basically the unspoken 'truth' that is required for your message to make sense. Here's an example.

When did you quit trying your best?

This question is designed to provoke an unpleasant response but also motivate someone to try harder in their efforts. The questions contain at least 7 separate presuppositions that are as follows:

1) It assumes that there was a time that you tried your best
2) That past results were better than the current results
3) You have now stopped trying your best
4) You can do better
5) You know that you could do better
6) That you are aware that you are not trying your best
7) You will answer this question

Answering the question in any way is to admit that you are not currently trying your best. If there is no good reason for the lapse in effort then you will quickly find yourself obligated to try harder next time. The only option here is to ignore the question entirely, this way the hidden presuppositions cannot infect your subconscious and take root in reality.

Write, Record, Repeat

The best way to create conversational language patterns is to write them down in the form of a list and running through them a few times a day. Don't spend hours on this exercise, just ten minutes or so once or twice a day will be more than enough to internalise the patterns. It is not enough to merely read and memorise the patterns, mix them up a bit, combine two, three or more of these patterns and create an entire conversation template. Try writing sentences and paragraphs that are made of as many Eriksonian type language patterns as possible and over time this will become so natural that you will start thinking in conversational language.

Familiarising yourself with the sound of your own voice is one of the fastest ways to progress and advance both your persuasive and listening skills. Record yourself saying the same few conversational language patterns over and over and pay close attention to any changes in tone and pitch. Practice these patterns until they sound congruent. By playing around with these new patterns, recording them and listening to them you will begin to develop your own particular style and through hundreds of repetitions, find hidden truths that lead to further depths and incites previously unthought of and from these possibilities will arise.

Get Started

At times creating our own conversational language patterns can appear problematic. It can be difficult to capture the essence of Eriksonian language, especially if we haven't properly considered our potential audience. But as with most things, a little practice brings quick results. By using the examples below alongside those mentioned earlier in this chapter you will be able to create numerous conversational language patterns to suit countless situations. Get used to the accommodating style of conversational language and practice when you can (never to the point of boredom) and in a short time, you will be gently influencing those around you in a most graceful and respectful way. A way which will also go completely unnoticed.

- Relaxation comes from within
- Look deep within
- If it feels right to you
- Concealed within
- Deeply moving
- It makes you wonder/you begin to wander
- Thought drift
- Twice rightly
- New perspectives drift into view
- Feel free to explore
- Whoever you are
- All avenues are open to expedition
- Comfortable concentration
- Deeper depths

- Now becoming
- The best of you
- Flow of thought
- Take to heart/in your heart of hearts

The Spoken Word

Words carry connections and associations which transcend the literal meaning of the word itself. Many commonly used phrases are associated with negative emotions and when overused such phrases can sometimes without notice, kick start unhelpful emotions, patterns, and behaviours. Ultimately, we think the way we speak and we use the same language patterns when speaking to others that we use when we communicate with ourselves internally. Therefore, as with so many of the methods and ideas discussed in these pages, we must first scrutinise ourselves in order to grasp a greater understanding of and influence over those we come into contact with. First, ask yourself:

What internal language, tone, pace, pitch, and volume do I use when I…..

- Congratulate myself
- Admonish myself
- Motivate myself
- Calm myself
- Relax
- Console myself
- Attack myself

What internal language, tone, pace, pitch, and volume accompany the following emotional states?

- Fear
- Anger
- Missing out

- Rejection
- Success
- Courage
- Justified
- Disgusted
- Compassion
- Wonder
- Excitement

What internal language, tone, pace, pitch, and volume do I use to:

- Convince myself
- Self-comfort
- Console myself
- Vent frustration

Speak the Language

By completing the exercise above you now have a list of how you are affected by words, tone, pace, volume. There will be variations from person to person but overall people are extremely similar in the ways in which language patterns affect them. For example:

- A slow speaking pattern with a gentle rhythm has a calming effect.

- Speaking in a choppy, high pitched fashion with erratic stops and starts will cause confusion and annoyance.

- A raised voice, sharp words and without pauses will cause anxiety or perhaps anger in others.

- Speaking from the sternum instead of the throat will create a confident tone which when used alongside a steady speaking rhythm with pauses used to create impact will motivate and convince others.

Using the information learned from analysing your own internal dialogue and how it affects you, you can adopt and adapt these patterns for eliciting specific emotional responses from others such as excitement, positivity or pessimism, solidarity, competence, trustworthiness and many more. The deeper your self-analysis goes the more patterns you will notice; these patterns are what governs much of human behaviour and generally form the underlying guidelines for communication alongside context and environment.

Take Control

Taking control of conversations and therefore situations can be done in a number of ways from the positioning of individuals, creating social barriers that block certain communications and even knowing and exploiting an individual's personal limitations to the mirroring, pacing and leading posture, tone, the and diction of NLP. Here, we are going to be covering ways in which words and language patterns can help us to gain the upper hand, as well as learning how our internal dialogue can be used to empower us as others use theirs to limit themselves.

Being competent, knowing it, and proving it are three very different things. When it comes to theoretical thinking most people believe themselves to be capable in the majority of situations, however, in the most part these theoretical situations never arise and so the imagined competency goes untested. The reality is that most people react badly to the unusual and unexpected, causing them to act in a knee jerk fashion. In the time between imagined competency and having that competency tested, individuals generally choose to make to with self-empowering internal dialogue (rather than any type of preparation, learning, or practice) to convince themselves that are able to weather any coming changes. When used alone like this empowering language can only lead to delusional behaviour and a rude awakening. On the other hand, when used correctly empowering language can support us by usurping negative internal dialogue like self-criticism and doubt. As we learn new skills, step into unknown territory, or debate especially difficult individuals.

Empowering language, or rather, empowering lines of questioning are particularly helpful if ever we fall short of our desired goals or receive unfavourable results. The following exercise has been designed to help you quickly get to the heart of an issue.

Be curious, look into your failings and emotional reactions. How might these current results and emotions help me to succeed, solve problems and find positive meanings and inspiration from this negative situation?

Ask yourself:

- Where does this current situation lead?
- What can I learn from this?
- How do I feel about this?
- How do I want to feel about it?
- What am I willing to do to feel this way?
- What can I learn from this?
- What is the next step?

Asking yourself the above questions will alleviate feelings of frustration, confusion, and powerlessness and reveal new options to you. You have in fact just taken back control of yourself.

Effecting Others with Language

We all want to get ahead in life. This means a lot of different things to a lot of different people, however, the basic need for water, food, shelter, and safety are universal and central to almost everything that anyone does, ever. Beyond the basic needs to stay alive are our social needs such as the need to feel understood and to be acknowledged. Following these social needs are the requirements for advancement i.e. education, innovation, teamwork, and planning. These life needs and social requirements all carry a huge number of linguistic connections and associations, many of which carry their own connotations both positive and negative. So, if the words we use carry associations that have the capacity to affect the emotions of those who hear them, and many of the needs affecting all of us have linguistic connections that can be presented in both negative and positive lights, we in fact have the choice whether to use language that will bring about a positive or negative impact. The important thing to remember here is to be aware of the emotional connections that certain words carry and to learn to recognise the accompanying emotions and preceding language patterns that lead up to and trigger emotional responses. Once we are aware of such things, we can guide people towards more positive and productive emotional states.

To fully grasp the power of words it is first important to understand its literal or denotative meaning as well as its emotional connotations. If you are not fully aware of the meanings and connotations contained within the words you use, your point may be lost and ignored as the inherent connotations often receive more attention than the point they are trying to substantiate. For example, if we look at the words employ, use and exploit. All three of them have pretty much the same literal meaning however the connotations they carry are often viewed very differently.

- Employ has a positive connotation. To be employed is generally viewed as a good thing as is to employ the correct tool or strategy.
- Similarly, use of or to use basically means the same, to employ. However, use carries a more neutral connotation.
- Whenever we see or hear the word exploit/exploited then someone has or is being used to their detriment and for the profits of others. When discussing those who have been or are being exploited, we are invariably discussing victims and so the word carries negative connotations.

Tone and Pace

Tone of voice is rarely used to full effect but the sad truth is that in reality, a great deal of information is portrayed through our tone, even more so than the words we choose to communicate with.

- A fast pace and high tone can indicate the speaker is tense, nervous or even scared.
- A neutral tone and slow pace can indicate boredom or sadness.
- A loud, erratic tone and pace indicates excitement and/or anger.
- A low volume and tone can indicate insecurities.
- A rhythmic pace and light tone can indicate happiness.
- A steady pace and the proper use of varying tone indicate confidence and competence.

When communicating with someone pay special attention to their tone of voice and try to discern their current underlying mood. Once you have an idea of their emotional state, choose a desired state. Then with subtly, closely match their tone and pace, follow on to slowly change your tone and pace in order to lead them to a new positive state.

The methods and techniques mentioned throughout this book should be practiced individually, one at a time until each one is second nature. At first, these skills will not come naturally but through practice, you will internalise them and be able to apply them singularly or combined in any way that suits the situation.

Understanding Each Other

Have you ever taken a moment to question how and why two people can share a conversation and each come away with completely different opinions on what was discussed and the outcomes derived from it? It is common for groups to share experiences only to later argue over the facts of what actually happened. How does this happen? The entirety of our lives is spent decoding the non-stop flow of information that our brains then use to create 'our' reality. However, our brains are limited in the amount of information it can focus on and process at any one time. The process the brain uses to choose what information to focus on largely unconscious and strongly connected to our preferences in using our bodily senses, visual, auditory, olfactory, kinaesthetic and gustatory. A good example is that one person may remember what was said and another person may remember what they saw whilst a third person may primarily remember how the event made them feel. Our brains log this information and create our 'reality' and then given meaning by the individual experiencing the event. Everyone processes information in their own unique way, with their own preferences and biases acting as influencing factors along the journey.

Most of the information thrown at us throughout the day is lost, missed or disregarded by our brains as useless, what is left is all the information we use to make our decisions. Once the brain has filtered through and logged all the information it is then filtered through our personality, ideals, and pre-conceptions and personal influencing factors including political, social, financial constraints, relationships, our view of ourselves and many more. Once processed these interpretations become fuel for out thought processes which in turn governs our emotional state.

To better understand others, we must view their current actions and emotional state as a starting point to truly understanding their thought processes and personal motivating factors. We must reverse engineer the behaviours and emotional state of others in order to effectively discern their thought process which will then lead us to the individual's personal interpretation of events, their immediate intentions, and motivating factors.

Once we know their motivating factors and beliefs, we can alter our approach accordingly. Speaking directly to an individual's personal beliefs is one of the most influential methods available to us. Not only are personal beliefs both reliable and excellent motivating factors but knowing and understanding how a person feels, believes and thinks will create an atmosphere of trust. When we communicate indirectly to a person's internal belief system, they will feel two things, that you truly know and understand them (this is incredibly powerful), and an irresistible call to action, both of which strengthen relationships and overall influence.

Once discerned, the simplest way to communicate a message directly to someone's internal beliefs and motivating factors is by storytelling.

Story Telling Skills

The ability to spin a good yarn has become a core business strategy over the past two decades. This prominent trend became popular through the rise of a need for brand recognition and as an attempt to curry loyalty with the customer. Nowadays, it's common practice for advertisers to create compelling stories about how their products or services first came to be, in the hopes of creating an emotional connection between consumer and product. When used properly this method has proven itself to be overwhelmingly powerful, so much so as to facilitate lifelong emotional bonds between consumers and their chosen product.

This type of storytelling should not be limited to just businesses advertisers and cleverly placed commercials. The art of brand building via storytelling can be applied to our own personal situations. For example, during a job interview, when asked about your previous roles, the ability to position yourself as an integral part of the framework of an interesting story will cause you to be remembered throughout the process and your application will receive greater attention and consideration.

Socially, telling a story is a great way to demonstrate that we are high-value individuals without openly blowing our own trumpet. A good way to do this is to tell a story of the exploits of a friend with yourself being just a small bit part player in the story, playing a role that portraits you in a light that supports your current role and objective.

The storyteller's diction, meaning the choice of words, tone, volume, and speed of speech are the tools with which the storyteller can establish a context, background and the story's process leading to a compelling conclusion. However, when we are telling a story in order to influence others it helps to start with the conclusion and fill in the background and key details later in the story, pitch, or presentation but if we are to maximise our influence it is important both begin and end with our primary message in the form of a conclusion.

We are all besieged by a seemingly never-ending torrent of information, most of which are either false or irrelevant and so people become desensitised and easily lose interest and concentration. It is for this reason that we must offer more than information alone, we must present that information in a way which instantly engages our audience both mentally and emotionally.

When we frame our key message as a logical conclusion, we must also give it an emotional charge that people can connect with. Speaking about facts 'emotionally' and using descriptive language designed to speak directly to the senses and emotions of the audience will greatly enhance the impact, rememberability, and overall influence of our message.

A core feature of NLP (Neuro-Linguistic Programming) is the theory that we all think in terms of our senses, and that we all have our preferences over which senses are dominant in our thought patterns. For those of us that think visually (a mental preference for in pictures) phrases like ", I see what you mean" will have a greater impact than, for example, "I grasp what you are saying". Below are a few examples of phrases that speak directly to the audience's senses:

Visual (Seeing)

- Big picture thinking
- I can see your point
- See the light
- I knew at first sight
- Can you picture it?
- See sense
- An idea with real scope and vision
- We don't want to leave anyone in the dark
- I can't see that happening
- Look to what we've already learned
- See what's ahead

Auditory (Hearing)

- I hear you loud and clear
- Let's hear each other out
- Loud and clear
- Let's tune in and get started
- I'm on the same wavelength
- He chimed in with his opinion
- It rings a bell
- The power of the spoken word
- It has a ring to it
- Sounds like a plan
- Their bark is worse than their bite

Kinaesthetically (Feeling)

- I've got a good feeling about this
- It's a good fit
- Something everyone can grasp
- Keep in touch
- Success is within touching distance
- It's within our reach
- I can almost touch it
- Feels like a weight has lifted
- Warm and friendly
- Break free from the icy grip of oppression
- I want everyone to feel comfortable
- Get in the swing of things
- He's a little rough around the edges
- If the shoe fits
- Strengthen your resolve

Olfactory (Smell)

- The sweet smell of victory
- I smell a rat
- Smells like trouble
- Something smells fishy

Gustatory (Taste)

- The taste of victory
- He comes across as bitter
- That idea leaves an awful taste in my mouth
- It's unpalatable
- We can no longer swallow this

Words to avoid

Some words are the unfortunate owners of such
negative connotations that it is best to completely
eliminate them for your everyday dialogue. Remember
these words, keep them locked away in your lexicon
and use them only in the most appropriate occasions,
ideally when their connotation is the point of your
communication. For example, using the word loser to
describe a friend or colleague, even as a joke is sure to
offend. However, if pitting two or more individuals
against each other, openly stating that there will be a
winner and there will also be losers (even if this is
already clear) will serve to spur on and motivate all the
individuals involved by stirring up an air of
competition. This method is particularly effective in
working environments.

If you are ever unsure of a word's connotation, write
it down alongside at least two other words with the
same or very similar literal/denotative meaning and
read them over a few times, paying special attention to
your emotional reaction to each word. Try using each
of the words within a sentence and note the effect each
of them has on the overall message portrait. Write
down the result and when the time comes you will have
the perfect words available to you to best suit your
purpose. Here are a few examples to get you started:

Negative-Neutral-Positive

- Unpopular-Specialised-Niche
- Stubborn-Determined-Steadfast

- Decrepit-Old-Vintage
- Stingy-Prudent-Shrewd
- Clique-Club-Alliance
- Delirious-Happy-Elated
- Critical-Choosy-Meticulous
- Intrusive-Curious-Inquisitive

Foul Language

It's always better to avoid foul language, it never works, unless you're looking for a cheap laugh around friends. It can't be denied that swearing and cuss words are widespread. We are surrounded by it; the habit is easily picked up and if we become comfortable with habitual swearing, we can inadvertently offend others without realising it. That is not to say that we should be offended by the swearing of others. If someone is emotional and using foul language then there is a good chance that there is at least a nugget of truth in what they are saying.

Common reasons why people swear:

- To vent frustration.
- To express anger.
- In order to appear brave or tough.
- To show defiance.
- Joining in with others.
- They think it will be funny.

Language Patterns and Literary Techniques

Particular language patterns, figurative language, and literary techniques are the tools of master communicators from actors to authors, comedians, teachers, marketers, and coaches of all kinds. When used effectively to convey emotion, heightened attention or imply deeper meaning, the impact of the message increases exponentially. Employing such methods allows us to quickly and easily make our message recognisable, memorable and distinct from the crowd. They help us to present our message in an audience-friendly way which arouses interest and slips past any negative preconceptions that others may hold. Once internalised we will connect and combine these methods to artfully outwit and convert any opposition by tailoring and presenting our directive in a way that suits the tastes and individual style of whoever we are communicating with. The following techniques are just a few common examples of literary techniques and language patterns that can be used in one to one interactions and written communications alike. They can be particularly useful in social media as often we need to create an impact in as few words as possible. The topic of language patterns, literary techniques, and their persuasive power will be covered in great depth in a later release from the *Secrets of The Dark Arts* series, however, below are some of the most useful and persuasive techniques that fit with the running theme of this book. That is to say that they are available to all and simple to both use and learn.

Allegory

An allegory is a story that has a double meaning, one that is outwardly expressed in the detailing of the story and another (usually the true meaning) hidden beneath the surface. Historically, this secondary meaning is a moral one, a lesson to live by from which we can learn. However, in our modern age, it is more common that these increasingly subliminal messages have a political or social meaning intended to influence our decision-making process and subsequent actions. A good example of this is the novel The Lord of The Flies by Nobel Prize-winning author William Golding, that at first seems like a tale of survival focussed on a group of school children, however, the underlying theme and message is of the primitive behaviours underlying our society and how fast we can descend into them when faced with our internal conflicting feelings regarding social organisation, rules, and personal status. The children represent more than mere children, they are society and the island itself is the entire world in which we live. Simply put an allegory is the moral of the story, the underlying message that is concealed within the narrative. The human brain evolved and survived through recognising patterns, connections, and associations in our immediate surroundings, and thousands of years later our brains still find it rewarding to analyse information in order to find the deeper meanings, patterns, and hidden truths. Using allegories is a safe and reliable way to inspire people and draw them to our cause, to call them to action, or to caution them from moving in a particular direction. It is also arguably the best way to give someone advice, because, as the narrative entertains the conscious mind the message hidden within the story slips past any conscious resistance and is absorbed by the subconscious where it can elicit emotions, create motivation, and increase the likelihood of action.

Alliteration

Alliteration, otherwise known as the repetitive use of consonant sounds at the start of words, is a subtle way to regain someone's attention mid-conversation without being direct. It doesn't have to be obvious and shouldn't sound contrived. Casually throwing a bit of alliteration into a conversation will stop listeners from getting bored and when used at the correct time, will add a ring of humour and intelligence to whatever point you are making. Well placed alliterations will stick in the mind of the listener and works particularly well with children and teenagers. An entire spectrum of marketing companies, advertisers, and slogans writers of all kinds use the power of alliteration to endear us to their products and services and cement them in our memories. Businesses the world over spend billions on marketing and the majority marketing campaigns are centred around smartly worded alliterations. The reason for this is because it works. So well in fact that everyone from best-selling authors of fairy tales to hard-core rap artists makes use of this effective language technique. Its powerful influence is commonly used as a sturdy foundation for nursery rhymes, children's stories, poetry, tongue twisters, popular music, and marketing campaigns. The persuasive power of alliterations is hidden in their ability to grab and hold the attention of others whilst simultaneously providing the listener with information in a way in which they are likely to remember. This ingenious technique instantly arrests the attention of the listener and effortlessly influences information retention. Fluid in fashion and fun to hear are two qualities that when combined, create a profound effect.

Here are a few basic examples of alliteration:

- Businesses benefit from busy bees
- Meticulous mathematicians make money
- Peter Piper picked a peck of pickled peppers
- Loose lips sink ships
- Blessed with a brilliant brain
- Candy creates cavities
- Grab the golden goose

Onomatopoeia

Imitate the source of the sound it is describing. These words make an incredible impact and should not be underestimated. The best examples of these are animal noises, however, they are not the most useful examples. Much better would be the likes of thud, bang, crash, pop, clash, whack, buzz, or squish. These words help to emphasise particular points and add emotion to boring conversations. Onomatopoeias are often used as pattern interrupts (more on this shortly) and double up as beautifully descriptive words which tend to help to maintain the focus of the listener.

Jargon

There's a reason that most people hate jargon, it tends to be the language of those who are either trying to dominate us in some way or those trying to convince of something that they themselves do not fully grasp. If something is true and reasonable it should be able to be explained within a few easy to understand eloquent sentences. However, this is not to say that jargon does not have its uses. Simply summing up the information might not always be enough to persuade others to join your standpoint and it is these times that following up with some jargon can be enough to cement your position. Ensure jargon is only used to bolster your position and strengthen your influence. For example, if someone is becoming emotional in opposition to your proposed methods or actions, hit them hard with jargon they are unlikely to understand upon first hearing and this will diffuse any emotional charge.

Ultimately, language techniques and other helpful speech patterns come to us in many shapes, sizes, and guises and can assist us in predicting and influencing the actions of others. Below is a brief recap of the above-mentioned language techniques and types of situations to which they are suited.

- **Alliteration** boosts the overall impact of our communication, enhances our likeability and grabs the attention of listeners. If you want someone to remember a specific piece of information, try using some subtle alliterations. Alongside alliteration, consider using **Assonance**. It is similar to alliteration; however, the vowel sounds are repeated (please abide and slide to the side). Assonance is slightly less poetic than alliteration but the effect is none the less influential.

- **Onomatopoeia** are descriptive words that sound like the source or the sound they are describing. They are perfect for use within metaphors and stories as they add another descriptive level to these already influential tools.

- **Jargon,** in addition, proves to be very effective when dealing with unruly individuals whose emotional state and lack of knowledge leave them struggling to justify their objections or behaviour. Calmly using 'business speak' and jargon against disruptive individuals will usually be enough to quell their rebellion and gain control of the situation. This is not limited to professional environments and works surprisingly well in less formal social interactions where its use is less expected.

The significance of being able to recognise language patterns cannot be understated as they are a key factor in letting us how another person is thinking and feeling and the way in which their emotional flow is heading.

Here are a few examples of the most effective ways to become familiar with language our own patterns

- Analyse your own language patterns and question yourself as to why do you use the words you choose?
- Write down and words, jokes or sayings that you use or hear regularly.
- Study popular culture for trigger words and overused references that most people would know.

Language patterns can be used to bring about a wide range of results. Eriksonian language is arguably one of the most effective language tools for influencing people ever devised. Eriksonian language, alongside many methods used by magicians and master manipulators alike, all contain high levels of suggestive language, that when used correctly can have a profound effect Therapists employ these hypnotherapy techniques to enact real and lasting changes in the lives of their clients the success of such techniques is undeniable and so warrants a closer look.

The purpose of loading communications with subtle suggestions is to convey specific ideas and inspire the desired action. Suggestive language is the bedrock of all influential linguistic techniques and is so irresistible that a great many industries have adopted them for use in everything from the job interview process to marketing campaigns and it has entirely taken over the direct sales industry.

Using suggestive language

Suggestive language should be viewed as fundamental to your overall level of influence. It is a skill which can be easily and endlessly improved and used instantly and often. When asking something of somebody a very popular method is to ask directly. Openly asking someone to do something for us may often work, but may often work isn't enough for us. When directly making a request or suggestion, wrap the direct suggestion with other subtle suggestions. The key to getting our suggestion heard is repetition, repetition, repetition. However, we don't want to beat our audience over the head or come across as a nag so this repetition must be done mainly through covert suggestions that are aimed directly at the subconscious. The idea is to communicate on many levels at once, this overloads the listener's conscious left brain thinking and information is allowed to flow directly into the more emotional and creative right hemisphere where it is likely to be accepted without any critical examination or evidence.

Here are a few examples of ways to become familiar with your own language patterns.

- Analyse your own language patterns and question yourself as to why do you use the words you choose?
- Write down and words, jokes or sayings that you use or hear regularly.
- Study popular culture for trigger words and overused references that most people would know.

Breaking A Pattern

Something as simple as an extended pause can be enough to break someone's train of thought for long enough for us to regain control of the conversation and therefore situation. A **Pattern Interrupt** is a term used by hypnotists to describe an action, phrase, sound or word that has the ability to break or disrupt an individual's current chain of thought or language pattern. The simplest example of this is the word No. The word No instantly breaks the mind away from its own flow and redirects attention back to the outside world.

Examples of pattern interrupt:

- "No"
- An extended pause
- A light touch on the shoulder
- Alliterations
- Assonance
- Onomatopoeias
- Jargon
- Raising the tone or pitch of our voices
- Visual cue such as a brightly coloured object

Break the Flow and Reframe

Once we have successfully interrupted someone's pattern of thought or thought process, we can quickly reframe the context and/or direction of the conversation. We disrupt someone's 'flow' by using unusual word patterns like alliterations and onomatopoeias, changes in the pitch and/or volume of our voice, or a known 'primer' (see Priming in Persuasion below) such as a visual cue. In the second intake for their brain to process the disruption, we begin reframing by first (in this particular example) setting the tone of our voice to one that is in line with our goal. This is where our storytelling skills come into play. Ideally, we want to reframe the situation in an interesting way, but in as few words as possible so that our audience does not get bored (this seriously diminishes our influence). One of the most fluid and natural ways to effectively reframe is through the art of storytelling. The rest of this chapter and much of the next chapter Persuasion can be used for reframing. All of the examples of stories/frames/styles below can be used in reframing to great effect. Finally, take special care to select the right story, one that best suits your desired outcome, and also one that will not tarnish your absolute influence or reputation.

The Underdog Effect

When we frame ourselves as the plucky underdog(s) it instantly triggers remarkably intense and long-lasting emotional responses in others. The theory behind it is that very few of us are giants, however, we all regularly find ourselves facing them. Everyone loves a champion, but what's better than a champion? A people's champion. A champion that has risen from the ranks of the populace, conquered adversity and defeated giants in order to proclaim victory will fast become a legend among men. Widely recognised and respected that the underdog rarely prevails through luck, quite the opposite, in fact, an underdog only succeeds through hard work, determination and more often than not against the odds. Underdogs have the reputation of being trustworthy, reliable, hard-working, law-abiding individuals, often working in line with the 'greater good' which inspires others to act, usually in the favour of the underdog. Framing yourself as the underdog will prove to be a reliable and powerful technique as it resonates with such a wide audience. Even superiors, 'higher-ups', and those more powerful than ourselves will regularly be inspired and motivated by the influential power of the underdog to act on our behalf. Here are a few examples of ways in which we can obtain the power of the underdog without facing overwhelming adversity:

- Project the image of the underdog by humbly portraying that you are willing to and have suffered for your cause or received unfair treatment in the pursuit of your most noble of goals. The key here is articulation, choose your words wisely to ensure you do not appear to be (making yourself) a victim and do not make any sweeping accusation or insults that may alienate those you are trying to rally to your cause.

- Telling both sides of the story in as unbiased a way as possible will project an air of honesty, credibility, and maintain your reputation as fair and balanced. All of which are essential if we are to effectively evoke the underdog effect.

- Underdogs do not use social media and spin to further their cause. To elicit the full force of the underdog effect we must do our persuading in person because a face to face conversation allows us to connect emotionally with our audience as well as giving us the opportunity to tailor our approach to that individual's values. Factoring the personal values and beliefs of our audience is a key aspect to keep in mind so that we can properly frame our 'message' in a way that speaks directly to either that person's emotions or values, or better yet both.

- Demonstrating courage, determination and persistence whilst remaining level headed will cause us to be viewed as tenacious individuals with both guts, intelligence, and stamina.

- Successful people rarely work alone and this is especially true for underdogs. The underdog effect effortlessly pulls people to you, it can covert the opposition simply by overcoming their previous logic with the intoxicating power of the underdog. Be a leader to those that follow your cause, be humble and understanding and you will be rewarded with faith and respect.

- Build an emotional connection with everyone you meet. The simplest way to do this is to search for an understanding that you share. If you can garner a mutual understanding between two individuals, even if they differ on opinion, a reciprocal trust will be formed. Provide value to all that you come into contact with both prior and post-converting to your cause, this will garner long lasted relationships.

- Be humble and likeable. These are two integral characteristics of the underdog. Do not be rash, never boast, and avoid pettiness at all cost as these behaviours obviate any gains achieved through the underdog effect. Reign in excessive passion and raised voices, both of which will cause you to be viewed as unpredictable and therefore unreliable which will alienate those around you who you wish to influence.

Let People Know They Hold Power

When we make a person aware of the power that they hold they are much more likely to see things your way and be willing to help in order to be the 'powerful character' they believe we see them as. As skilled leaders and masters of persuasion we only truly rely on our own abilities, however, creating and working with a team of competent collaborators speeds up the process and takes some of the weight of our shoulders. Let people know exactly why you need them, their experience, their individual characteristics, and strengths. Terms like 'we'll be at a loss without you' and 'your abilities make you the ideal person….' Will let people know that you value them and understand their skill set. Appeal to their professional pride, throw in a dash of implied superiority and your colleagues will be yours to command.

It's Not A Test

When we are trying to influence someone, we are in one way or another attempting to educate and inform others. We all need to be understood, even more so if we are hoping to persuade and influence others. However, often we want others to understand the full extent we have gone to for our cause and the depth of our newly obtained knowledge or plans but we resist. Our aims are towards influencing others not educating them or gaining their admiration, so keep it short, keep it sweet, and appeal to key points.

Make Them Feel Smart

If we can frame our message and the detailed information contained within in a way that allows the audience to see how smart they are. Don't spend too long extensively discussing each point or every equation applicable to the numbers, briefly touch the elements that either adds credibility your ideas or cannot be ignored. Focus on explaining what the evidence means, not the evidence itself, this will cause your audience to focus on the meaning and the potential impact of the data instead of the individual aspects that lead to your conclusion. This method of reframing allows others to except a lot of information on very little evidence and saves us a lot of time. Appealing to someone's intelligence is a very effective strategy.

Using Negative Humour

Negative humour is typically associated with obnoxious individuals and as an overused tool of bullies everywhere. In reality negative humour, when used at the right time to poke fun at ourselves, often makes us come across as well rounded, trustworthy individuals.

Be sure only to use negative/self-deprecating humour when dealing with equals or subordinates. In the eyes of superiors, self-deprecative humour will cause you to be viewed as lacking in confidence, however, it has the opposite effect in more relaxed social settings, for instance when used in conversation with subordinates, work colleagues, team members, and friends. To these people, your negative humour will come across as a mix of confidence, modesty, and good humour. This will add to your credibility, likeability, and trustworthiness, and significantly strengthen your overall influence.

The Five Single Most Influential Words in The English Language

"You", or your name is the powerful word that can be used against you, it is like music to your ears. Saying someone's name is incredibly influential, exceedingly simple, and above all suspicion. Never forget to call people by their name as often as possible.

It's usually what comes after the word **Because** that makes it so influential. Giving any reason at all has been proved to be much more influential than giving one at all. Even a thinly veiled reason will convince some people, two or three reasons in a row should be enough to break most individual's resistance.

Instantly/Now/Faster/Immediately are grouped together here as they all evoke very similar mental and emotional responses. We hear these words and our brains light up, especially if we are to receive immediate gains. If something can be acted on instantly it often will be, even more so if it can be framed in a positive light using skills from the Persuasion chapter below.

Simply put, **New** is often equated with better. Our feelings towards the things we buy of deteriorate faster than the item itself. The car finance industry is an ideal example. Every year, tens of thousands of individuals go into debt which they can barely repay, to buy new cars that they don't need in order to impress people who don't care. Why? Because they perceive new as better. Ultimately this is a sign of inner issues concerning self-worth and trying to fill that metaphorical hole with material possessions, a pastime which has become epidemic in the past decade.

We automatically avoid loss, no one wants to lose out or be left with less than they started with. The word **Free** triggers emotions that are surprisingly close to the fear of losing out and so it causes us to act fast in order to ensure that we don't lose out or get left o

Conmen

Conmen, especially those of the early 20th century possessed persuasive skills bordering on the sublime. The escapades of legendary characters like Frank William Abagnale, Victor Lustig, and Joseph 'Yellow Kid' Weil are all packed full methods that exploit the human condition. These players were nothing short of masterful in their knowledge of human nature and the ways in which they manipulated and provoked their marks is nothing short of supernatural. In this chapter, you will learn of some of the most cunning, daring, and bold cons in history as well as what made them work and why. These real-life examples of accomplished con artists (they're called artists for a reason) will inspire your actions and shed light on the true lengths people will go to when their critical thinking skills have been interrupted and distorted with ideas of power and greed. The methods and audacity employed by such men as "Soapy" Smith and Charles Ponzi had enough longevity that lasted long past their lifetimes and although the delivery of their techniques may have changed over the years many of them are still in use to this day. The stories and example mentioned below will allow you to recognise these types of scams when they present themselves in their present, which they will. Each example will point out specific motivating factors and weaknesses in the mark which led to their downfall, as well as the approach used by the conman to successfully pull off the scam.

The Man Who Sold the Eiffel Tower

In 1925 Victor Lustig (1890-1947), posing as an official from the French government called together a group of wealthy metal traders in a Parisian hotel. In this most confidential of meetings, it was said that due to the damage, ware, and rust plaguing the Eiffel Tower it had been decided by the French government that it would be broken down and sold off for scrap at a fraction of the 'scrap' value. This was because the maintenance costs for the tower could not be justified in such a trying economy and that the government's coffers were running low and could do with the significant boost that the sale of the tower would bring. Sure, some of the metal merchants were wary of the validity of this spectacular offer. However, once the ever-astute Victor Lustig hinted that he would require a bribe for his part in the transaction, all worries were put to rest as asking for a bride was common practice for government officials of the time. Once the bribe and payments for the tower had been made Victor Lustig disappeared, of course, only to surface to play the con again and he remains the only man to have sold the Eiffel Tower twice. The key factor Victor Lustig acted upon in this con was greed and he played greed as a card twofold. Firstly, he appealed to the greed of the metal dealers, offering them an excellent deal that would not only make them a lot of money but would also make them famous, leaving their mark on history as the men who purchased the Eiffel Tower. Secondly, in asking for a bribe he allowed the metal trader who paid it to believe he could see that his true intentions in facilitating such a deal were first and foremost, self-motivated greed. Victor Lustig's apparent greed rang true with the metal merchant's own greed and so he trusted him and lost his money on what is known as one of the most spectacular scams in history.

Soap Star

For over two decades Jefferson Randall Smith (1860-1898) ran a particularly innocent-seeming scam called 'The Prize Soap Racket'. 'Soapy' would roll into town selling bars of soap for 1$ apiece and make the claim that hidden within his inventory of regular soap was a bar containing a 100$ bill. The bar of soap containing the 100$ had of course been given to a mole hidden amongst the crowd who was set to reveal 'his' prize bar, claiming that he had won, only once a sufficient amount of regular old soap bars had been purchased by the gathering crowd. Once word spread, greed fuelled buying frenzies soon broke out making Soapy a nice profit. The scam ran successfully for twenty years due to its mix of social proof and implanting in others the idea that they can buy a 100$ bill with 1$. Once the public started telling each other about this guy they saw win 100$ from a 1$ bar of soap most of Soapy's work had been done for him. Crowds would seek him out in order to buy soap much in the same way people buy lotto tickets today, and of course, no one but Soapy ever won a dime.

Landmark Trader

George Parker (1870-1936) is, without doubt, the undisputed champion of 'selling' landmarks and public buildings and he did so repeatedly until his third conviction in 1928, and subsequent life sentence. George would approach wealthy immigrants while posing as a bored bridge builder and current owner of the Brooklyn Bridge. He wanted to sell the bridge quickly and was willing to accommodate low-ball offers in order to get a deal finalised so that he could go back to what he loved doing most, building bridges. The proposal would even have a ready-made money-making strategy for the buyer included. By charging a toll to those crossing the bridge the new owners of the Brooklyn Bridge would recoup their modest investment in next to no time. In addition to selling the Brooklyn Bridge a reported twice a week for years on end he also 'sold' off the tomb of Ulysses S. Grant, the original Madison Square Garden, The Metropolitan Museum of Art, and even the Statue of Liberty. The reason that selling the Brooklyn bridge worked so well and so often was due to two main factors. First of all, George was friends with (and bribed) a number of ferry and ship stewards in order to find out which of the passengers were both wealthy and new to the United States. Once George had the knowledge of who had the money, where they were from and preferably how they made their fortune he would tailor an appropriate approach and then propose an offer that was too good to miss and let their greed and imagination take over. The other reason the selling of the Brooklyn Bridge, in particular, was so successful is that publicly there was a dispute as to who actually owned the bridge, was it Brooklyn or Manhattan? George filled in the grey area and stated that it was actually himself who was the current owner and he was looking for a quick sale so he could move on. George chose his victims carefully, committing time and money to his due diligence and sought out those who nothing about the United States except that it was the 'land of opportunity'.

The Scam King

Joseph Weil (1875-1976), popularly known as 'Yellow Kid' is regarded as one of the most successful confidence in history. He made a reported $8 million operating all kinds of scams, fixed betting and the selling of non-existent property, land and oil deals to name just a few of his better-known examples. One day, a wealthy Canadian businessman caught wind of an opportunity through a certain Fred Buckminster. The owner of the National Commercial Bank had recently discovered oil and wished to sell off the land along with its massive oil deposits, with the one catch being that it must be sold via cash transaction in a bid to avoid taxation. This appealed to the Canadian, as a wealthy man himself he knew only too well the pains of taxes for the rich. And so, a meeting was scheduled to be held at the National Bank itself. Here, the security of the cash (half a million dollars) could be guaranteed and the necessary documentation could be properly inspected before changing hands. On the day of the scheduled meeting the bank happened to be very busy, the extra security caused a delay, the landowner was late and our Canadian was beginning to show his annoyance, at which point the landowner appears carrying all the proper information and documentation to finalise the deal. There was a last-minute negotiation made by the Canadian which cost the landowner made a concession $100,000 but he was happy to accept $400,000 and be on his way and the Canadian left the bank feeling like a baron. Soon enough though the Canadian realised that the land and its oil were phony and upon returning the bank he found it completely closed down. This is perhaps his best-known enterprise and is known as 'the one-hour bank'. Upon hearing that the National Commercial Bank was relocating its offices, Yellow Kid had approached the owner and rented one of the soon to be empty offices at the bank. The very same day that the bank moved the Canadian businessman arrived to complete the deal of a lifetime. The scope of the scam is incredible, the entire bank was set up as a working bank in order to solidify the trust of the businessman. The unexpected delays were designed to frustrate the Canadian and draw his attention from the fine details of the workings of the bank and the $100,000 last minute concession added a dose of superiority to the attitude of the Canadian, the results of which left him completely blind to the scam happening all around him. Fuel someone's feelings of greed and lead them to a set stage and they will play the part you have scripted for them. Stalling for time, provokes emotions and distorts the decision-making process which will reveal previously unnoticed opportunities for you to exploit.

History's Greatest Imposter

Frank William Abagnale Jr (b.1948) started his career early, at the age of 15. By the time of his arrest at age 21 he had at least 8 alias' was a master of both forgery and fraud and had successfully impersonated many professionals including prison officials, teachers, lawyers, doctors, and most famously an airline pilot on many occasions. This man operated with such confidence that he was able to take the bar exam three times and travelled an approximate 1,000,000 during his exploits as a commercial airline pilot. Using well prepared and cleverly forged paperwork Frank would open bank accounts under false names and write a number of cheques, cash them in a skip town before the bank realised, this scam continued for years while Abagnale travelled the world 'deadheading' as an airline pilot. Most of Abagnale's cons come down to a combination of planning and larger than life boldness that allowed him to effortlessly adopt any guise necessary when it came to getting what he wanted.

The Art of Persuasion

Persuasion as an art should be subtle and unnoticed. Less forceful than manipulation, more palatable than coercion, persuasion carries with it the assumption that, those persuaded act out of their own 'fully informed' will and usually in a way that works towards the embitterment of all involved. This is not necessarily the case, however, framing an idea in an altruistic way of thinking is a good place to start. The following methods of persuasion are focussed on being passive in our persuasion, we wait for the right time, consider their feelings, their values and standpoints. These tactics compliment and support each other to create a strategy that is practically impossible to see through and so cannot be directly argued against or attacked with violating socially agreed upon rules of conduct.

- Using an honourable cause is a great way to get someone's attention but an honourable cause alone is rarely enough to convert others to your way of thinking, to truly convert them we must shift their focus away from the cause to their own self-interest. Linking a great cause to the self-interest of listeners is an overwhelmingly powerful motivator. Once the listener begins to think about what they may get out of modifying their opinions or reassessing their loyalties the cage door is closed.

- As a rule, anyone can be persuaded of anything providing the timing, approach and context are correct but there are limitations such as time constraints. Prior to any attempt at persuasion, analyse the context of the situation as a whole and devise an approach that is acceptable and based around the current underlying mood or general atmosphere, otherwise known as the emotional 'flow' of the situation. Do not go against the flow of the situation, instead use the emotional flow to your advantage. Frame your ideas as exciting when people are jovial and as safe and pre-emptive in times of reflection. Going with the flow in this way allows you to syphon the already existing emotions in the room directly into your initiative. This method is ultimately more effective than simple trying to change the topic of conversation to one that serves your purpose.

- Timing is another pivotal factor when persuading others. The time of day greatly affects the expected desires of any particular person, for example, if we try to corner someone at work at 4pm on a Friday afternoon it is likely that all they can think about is leaving work for the weekend and so a large part of their brain will have already left the building. This could work to our advantage or against it depending on the goal. The timing of an approach extends beyond hours and days to weeks, months, and years, the longer ahead we can plan the greater our overall chances of success.

- Identify those individuals who are 'on the fence' or easy to influence and concentrate your efforts on these individuals in the same way that politicians focus on 'swing' voters.
- Most people are their own worst enemy, give them enough rope and they will only be too happy to tie the noose. Ask questions that get people talking and they will quickly voice opinions and values that can then be mirrored back at them in the present or used at a later date to obtain their consent. Being cordial will cause people to open up to you and in doing so they will provide the information needed to devise an approach that speaks directly to their personally held beliefs and values, at which point they will be powerless to refuse you or refute your way of thinking.

Do's and Don'ts of Arguments

We should be able to avoid most conflicts through clever manoeuvring and planning but there will be times when unpredictable people and event s catch us off guard and we are forced to either publicly or privately defend our position. By not instigating such situations we automatically begin in a position of power from which we can choose exactly how to respond and set the tone for the rest of the interaction. If someone is attempting to start an argument or becoming abusive it is likely caused by uncontrolled emotions which implies that they have not and are not planning ahead. There are a number of ways to use this to your convenience from passively listening (in order to obtain ammo) to deliberate provocation (to cause someone to lose their temper) and from simple distraction to appealing to values, all have their benefits, although some methods such as baiting someone into a temper tantrum will not win over your opponent and should only be used when attempting to influence the audience and as a last resort. The tips in this chapter include actions and behaviours that should be avoided due to blatant nature and their futility and the detrimental effect they have influence and persuasion.

Do

Keep cool

It's easy to become caught up in a passionate moment or to feel frustration when faced with an argumentative and unreasonable individual. However, even a momentary lapse in composure can set us back massively and it also gives those with an eye to, an opening to exploit. We do not need to restrain ourselves to the point that we are far removed, in fact, a little of emotion helps keep the thought process flowing. It is a matter of balance; we must place ourselves somewhere between stoicism and enthusiasm without emotionally engaging any other individual or their point of opinion. Do not resist the arguments of others, seek to augment them to your purpose by playing the long game, always be aware of the end goal, and remember that losing your temper is a sign of powerlessness.

Use slick one-liners whenever possible

Cleverly placed, hard-hitting one-liners have the ability to completely throw a person's chain of thought. A smart cliché or witty observation can completely demotivate an opponent for a few seconds, enough time for you to take control of the interaction. These seemingly spontaneous and intelligent interjections need not always make clear sense but be sure to sound reasonably sincere, you do not want to be seen as a heckler needlessly interrupting the flow of an otherwise relevant conversation. Here are a few of my favourite examples:

- Don't you think this will come back to bite us?
- Right or wrong, it's still beside the point.
- But what does that mean in the real world?
- What exactly are the parameters?
- You seem defensive?
- You're comparing oranges and apples.
- What research did you do?

Use tactical contradiction

When discussing matters in front of an audience it is possible to convert those who are still undecided by dissecting and contradicting specific points of your opponent's proposal. By contradicting them we have an opportunity to discredit their entire initiative, even the points that are 'airtight' can be undermined through the association with premises that can be proved faulty or even better, foolish. Don't be afraid of a little humour bordering on the theatrical, the audience will enjoy it, however, take care not to get carried away and become disruptive to proceedings.

Make an appeal

From time to time, you will find yourself in a situation where you have exhausted your logic, expertise, and powers of persuasion. When this happens, it is no doubt due to the fact that we missed a step along the way leaving the listener/audience room for critical thinking. It is almost impossible to immediately reverse engineer the interaction and start over and mush in the same way that it is easier to win a new chess game than it is to recover one after a few poorly considered moves. In these cases, we can appeal to higher values which will buy us valuable thinking time and also strengthen our position so that we can then reapproach the issues from a slightly different angle by following up with some questions like:

"Don't you think that this would make things safer for everyone involved?"

"Shouldn't we be working together on this?"

"Yes, but, what kind of world do we want to leave for our children?"

Practice pinpoint listening skills

People get emotional when they speak and because of this, they make slip-ups, huge ones. Many people are terrified of speaking in front of others and those who are not afraid of public oration are often overly confident, in either themselves or their message. By intently listening to someone we will at once be aware of their emotions, we can choose to 'pump' these emotions with questions directed to either excite or annoy. At this point, by pretending that you will concede a good point if only they see your point of view, they are likely to openly agree with you. The instant they do, undermine or contradict their point or objective. This simple '*bait and switch*' technique will leave the opposition annoyed and confused, allowing you to take control and move on to other issues in the assumption that you have won this time. The people present will assume the same and when the opposition sense this they will internally admit defeat rather than go against the group consensus.

Play Devils' advocate

By playing the part of the Devil's advocate we can infuriate our opponent, prodding them until they lose their composure and the debate. Playing Devil's advocate consists of gently arguing against and questioning an idea relentlessly, even if we secretly agree with the point being made. It is a tactic that can also be used on your own ideas. Question yourself in the way that you believe an incessantly annoying sceptic would and bolster the foundation of your position and find better ways to protect and strengthen it. Doing so builds resistance to the negative comments, needless questioning, and behaviour of others which so often drains many of us of our creative juices and sometimes even confidence. When playing Devil's advocate in order to annoy an opponent do so with a hint of ridicule and ask questions that severely stretch the premise of your opponent's position until the distortion causes it to appear absurd.

Don'ts

Indulge distractions

Sceptics, disbelievers, and dissenters will often try to distract you with phoney and half-hearted arguments and the truly argumentative may even attempt to push extreme examples of your ideas in order to distort them so that they seem ridicules or even reckless in the hopes of either redirecting your argument or causing you to lose your composure. Avoiding such distractions is not always easy, especially the ones that carry an emotional edge but by being firm and focussed you can avoid deviations like digressions and subject changes. Resist the urge to dismiss or stifle others, allowing others to opine is essential in so many ways, thank them for their valued input and Segway through some connection or other back to your original point, ideally using the interjection to strengthen your own ideas.

Make personal attacks

Lowering yourself and making personal attacks won't win advocates or arguments. You won't convert a person you've just offended, and anyone else present will automatically assume that your ideas as well as your integrity lack substance. We already know not to attempt coercion or persuasion, or enter into negotiations without being properly prepared and for this reason we can assume that if you are engaged in debate it is because to do so serves your purpose in some way, it can also be assumed that losing both the argument and the respect of those present is not part of the plan and therefore in no circumstance give in to the temptation of making abusive comments. If someone attacks you in this way, stay calm but express your surprise and disappointment that someone would act such a way towards a close friend (colleague works just as well) and make a confident request to "deal with the issue at hand rather than antagonise each other".

Use weak arguments

Some people like to present every possible piece of evidence that supports their case in the hopes of making their argument completely irrefutable. The problem is that doing often overloads the audience who quickly lose enthusiasm along with interest and a significant amount if the message's impact is lost. It is absolutely correct to research any and all factors that either add strength to or expose weaknesses in your plans. However, presenting all of this information to others will overload them, the mediocre points will diminish the more important ones and the audience will likely be unsure as to exactly what point you are trying to make. Use two or three factors that you believe will captivate and motivate your targeted audience and start there. If your best examples do not convince them, it is very unlikely that the mediocre ones will. If this is the case, adapt your strategy.

Covert Persuasion Techniques

The following strategies and tactics are not intended to be golden rules yet their dependability in the real world is reassuringly strong. The methods discussed in this chapter should go completely unnoticed by your targets and should never be revealed less all influence be immediately 'watered down'. Practicing covert persuasion is incredibly enjoyable, much in the same way as people watching, but we give them a slight push here and there depending on our objective. The aim of the game is to get the target to shift perspective, and sometimes loyalties without them knowing. It is not always the case that the audience is unaware of the persuasion, complete obliviousness is not necessary as many people savour the feeling of being led. If they ever happen to consciously recognise what you are doing it will in most cases have already occurred and the insight will be in retrospect and so can be addressed separately.

Resistance

Resistance is something that most of us dread, especially in social settings, but in truth, most resistance can be easily and simply neutralised, in a lot of cases before it even raises its ugly head. With a little forethought and insight, we can take the edge off of any resistance and at times even use it to our advantage.

If you have reason to believe that you will face resistance, there are a number of ways to subdue it, for example, employing distractions like mentioning quotes by one of their heroes or a well-known and respected authority figure, one that they daren't publicly refute.

Another way of redirecting resistance as it arises is to enact an immediate context change, completely ignoring what was about to be said. This instant change in direction will momentarily confuse the listener as they try to register it, they will take a second or two to question whether they have missed something. This momentary internal reflection will disrupt their thought pattern for long enough for you to capitalise, take control of the interaction, cement your position and move on to another topic of discussion.

Weaponised Agreement

Agreeing as much as possible without hurting your position can be used to soften your opponent's reserve allowing you to slip crucial details past without notice. It is similar to the distraction method mentioned above, however, acting agreeable has a much wider scope and can be adapted to most situations. Affirm the person's values and praise their wise opinions, but be sure that you can connect them to your own actions and ideas, once they acknowledge and accept your praise, they are in fact closing the door on any chance they had at refusing your ideas without violating their own values.

Cycle Back to the Target's Objectives

The more you can associate your initiative with the interests of others the more advocates you will acquire. Even if your goal doesn't directly affect your target's, speaking of the moral connection or values attached will create associations that siphon their emotional bond from the audiences' own hopes and dreams. You must be seen to honour and respect the opinions and wishes of others and if you do so in a way that incorporates your desired outcome it will be extremely difficult for anyone to muster an effective opposition that does not violate their own values and alienate at least some of the opinions of the group.

Manipulate 'Peaks' to Subdue Opponents

If we sense that someone is leading up to a good point we can wait for the perfect moment and opine or distract in order to throw the speaker off of their flow and so lessen the overall impact of their message. If we can subtly question and delay the speaker for long enough the intended message will be distorted and perhaps not voiced at all. When an audience is attentive and you can see the speaker is about to hit a 'home run', innocently but confidently interject, pump the emotion of the listeners and divert that energy towards your own goal.

During one to one interactions, we can choose words that will placate or frustrate our counterpart depending on our objective. Reading the ebb and flow of a person's emotions as they tell their 'story' and either obstructing or indulging them as to steer them in a direction of our choosing is as ingenious as it is indirect and, in most cases, will go totally unnoticed, at least until after the fact.

Wording

Slight nuances in wording work very much in the same way that leverage works to lift previously unmovable objects. Our choice of words is particularly important when we want to say no to someone in a way that will be both accepted and not offend. For example, the most common word used by people when turning down a request is can't. The problem with the word can't is that people typically believe that this can't, with a little persistence, could be turned into a can. This will invite challenges to your position which will require firmness and wasted time and energy to turn down. Instead, try using "I don't have time" or "I don't do that" the next time that you need to tell someone no as this makes no challenge and leaves no avenue for conversion.

There will be times when we are dealing with someone who is fixated on an issue to the detriment of everything else. Perhaps they are disrupting others or simply wasting time in the face of a deadline. Either way, there are ways of handling such situations without being forceful. What you need to do at times like these is to shift the attention of the individual, even if only momentarily to where we want it to be, this is done through an overt but passive statement. We can then follow up by asking a simple question which through answering, causes them to creatively enter into your premise. This subtle tactic causes an internal shift in emotion, which is then followed by the corresponding action. Here's a simplified example:

- "The real concern is not whether the dress looks flattering on you, which it so clearly does, but whether or not we're going to make it to the reception on time.
- Followed up by an innocent question, "Will you be ok sitting at the back? I mean we'll still be able to see the ceremony"

This method shifts attention from the present to the upcoming event, which will carry its own motivations, such as arriving on time. You have just indirectly made your point.

Bait and switch

This is another technique that works brilliantly with divisive and disagreeable individuals. Prior to initiating conversation prepare a casual question or statement designed to elicit either agreement or resistance (depending on whether the individual in question is more motivated by moving towards pleasure or moving away from pain), we can use the momentum of the agreement/resistance later, if there is any kickback to our next move. At this point we make our request or put forward our idea, framing it as connected to what our target has just stated they agree with or opposed to the concepts they have just rejected. If they show resistance, use the target individual's own wording (used in the previous agreement/resistance) to summarise your idea and the ways in which it supports the values that your listener has just claimed to hold. People find it very difficult to disagree with their own words (especially if spoken only moments before), this is why baiting someone into stating their position or personal beliefs and then switching out the original context or subject, seemingly in order to prove the universal truth of your target's wisdom is so powerful. Once this (predicted and elicited) wisdom is enthusiastically combined with your desired outcome you then instantly attribute this 'new found' flash of inspiration to your target's insight, at this point there is little chance of disagreement, I mean, who is going to disagree with someone telling them how insightful and wise they are?

Lazy is Not A Problem

Everyone loves a short cut, as a species we habitually follow the path with least resistance, preferring the easy route to one perceived as unfavourable or difficult. Typically, if there is no obvious consequence of taking no action whatsoever people will sit there gathering dust for extended periods of time. At first glance this attitude may seem troublesome for the persuader, however, the opposite is true. All you need to do to persuade a lazy individual and motivate them to action is to frame your ideas as easier when compared to the alternative and throw a small list of problems that are avoided as a side effect of your proposal. Emphasise the fluidity and simplicity of your plan, alongside how little input is required, its efficiency, speed of completion and lasting effects and there will be little denying your proposed course of action.

Tasks and Timescales

Procrastination, boondoggling, and blatant timewasting are traits that we all no doubt recognise and suffer from to some degree. It's annoying to us to see someone wasting time at a task we ourselves could have complete in half the time and one of the reasons this happens so regularly is that the other person has no idea what the expected time frame is in which the task should be completed. Straight out telling someone that this or that should be completed in X amount of time will likely cause resistance and so it is much more effective to be indirect and ask them how long do they think it will take them to get the job done. Let them know that a lesser peer would be expected to complete the task in however long you believe the task should fairly take to finish. The fact that you are now speaking to the individual as if they are 'higher up the chain' will in most cases have them confidently stating that they will accomplish the task in a quicker timeframe than expected. Once the individual has stated their expected timeframe, they will have invested themselves in meeting it and the timewasting won't be an option.

Credit Where It's Not Due

If someone is wrong about something, we assume that once enlightened with better information they will graciously change their mind. However, the opposite is usually the case. People don't like to be told they are wrong, and when told so, their logical thinking often ceases and emotional reactions take over, and as a result, they hold on to their position as if their lives depended on it. People often react to what they anticipate is going to happen, for example, if someone senses that your point is going to discredit them, they will have an emotional reaction, perhaps shame or a slight humiliation, which causes them to reject your proposal outright in order to stop that from happening. They don't care about the facts; they only want to protect their fragile emotions. The way around this is to attribute credit and give praises where it isn't necessarily due when it hasn't really been earnt but doing so entangle others in your persuasion. Structure your words as if your opponent is never wrong, there is in fact the inspiration for your greater initiatives and you will make sure that no one ever forgets it. Receiving such praise and recognition for doing so little is very alluring bait and will bring you many allies.

Begin with what they believe

Paying respect to facts and opinions that you know a person already believes can be used to create a solid foundation for covert persuasion. When attention is placed on a distinct idea or value the brain is sensitive to information that supports it, and so is more susceptible to influence if it embodies or reinforces the previously held belief in some way. Begin with what someone already believes to be true, shift the sentiment towards your new proposal (a proposal that holds values relating to or reflecting the belief), summarise and take a step back, allow the target to make their own final conclusions, conclusions that support your desired outcome. Once the connection has been made, they will at the very least feel that they have to agree with your proposed course of action to avoid feeling like a hypocritic.

False memories

Say that you heard about an event or occurrence from a trusted friend, work superior, family member and that you'd love to hear their side of the events. Ask what they saw at the time, what stood out, how they felt about specific happenings within the event. The most surprising thing about questioning people in this way is that most people will answer your questions. The brain has the ability to create false memories which can then be drawn from when questioned by a skilled inquirer. If we do this at the correct time (at a crucial point in a negotiation, or another semi-busy atmosphere works best), we can instantly gain support for our ideas, ideas that conveniently resonate with the values and emotions associated with the newly implanted false memory. It's not that someone will suddenly 'remember' entire narratives, surrounding and those who were present. We must coax the false memory into creation by drip feeding important elements and then asking the person questions relating directly to the information we just gave them. Most of us think using a collection of words and images that together create meaning from sounds, symbols, emotions, etc, and it is because of this that the brain creates images as the person searches their memory in order to answer our question. If they seem unsure add more information, quote someone who was there. Add a subtext to the false memory that allows the person being questioned to feel superior in some way, this will give their brain a reason to engage creatively. Once the individual begins to answer questions by utilising the false memory the more questions, we ask the more the memory is supported we can link it to your current proposal, strengthening both in the process. We cannot implant memories of entire trips or large-scale events but we have no need to as we only desire to influence the immediate decisions and actions of our target and that is can be achieved with vague false memories of past conversations and passing comments. Adding extra aspects to events that did in fact happen is an excellent way of achieving this effect. Most people are rarely 100% present to current proceedings, so asking them to remember fictional aspects of conversations that did actually happen is surprisingly easy, all we need do is enter into the conversation with confidence and innocence, ask a few questions and let that person's creative process do the rest. This technique is great for guiding people towards a desired standpoint or decision, and one that they will believe to be entirely their own making.

Suggestibility is an ever-moving spectrum, at certain times, in specific environments, and during certain events, you will find people to be more or less suggestible. However, it is a fact that some people are just naturally disagreeable, sceptical, or resistant to suggestibility, and so the above-mentioned method cannot be applied to every single case. Although, if the false memory is subtle, perhaps a slight tweak on the actual flow of real events, one that seems plausible, and also (if true) would show the target in a positive light, even the least suggestible person will at least consider what you are saying, and may go along with it anyway in order to either, make you happy, avoid confrontation, because it seems easier, they may agree with your overall premise, succumb to peer pressure, they can't fully remember the true event, simply can't think of anything better, or any number of personal reasons.

Envision a glorious future

Once the brain begins to create visual images associated with a new idea or action that idea will instantly cause a corresponding emotional reaction to what they anticipate will be the reality of the idea or action. With the use of descriptive language and a captivating style, a vision can be created of a bright future filled with praise and success. By stating what the benefits of your proposal in a descriptive way will mean for the future and how it will positively affect them, you allow the listener to creative licence to interpret what this will mean for their day to day lives. This will create a vision of the future full of possibilities and internal associations that we, the influencer will not be aware of. Ask a few loaded questions such as "what will you do with all your new found free time once X is implemented?" Once they answer the deal is pretty much sealed and so we can move on to our next agenda.

The Illusion of Choice

When seeking agreement, creating the illusion of choice is a proven way to engage people and provide them with a feeling of being valued in the decision-making process. When we seemingly defer to another person and let them know that we value their opinion they will often only be too happy to pick one of the choices you have laid out for them. Ask them to elaborate on their reasons and request their constructive criticism on the rejected ideas. People are eager for this type of attention, and will in most cases be as enthusiastic as they are unaware of what you are doing. Once our target makes their choice, congratulate them on their reasoning and you will not only have covertly persuaded them but also gained a reliable supporter to the cause.

Don't Overshoot Your Mark

What's said last is often remembered longest, this is the crux of why continuing past the point of victory can quickly lessen the impact of the victory and just as swiftly turn it into a defeat. Once your position is secure, it is wise to back off and re-evaluate. Allowing the emotion and momentum of a victory to push you past your mark puts you in uncharted territory without a clear path and without anything except experience to carry you through. In most instances a little logic combined with some experience is enough to get by in life, but, in the game of power and persuasion, the most essential ingredient for success is the planning and research we put into each new project prior to taking any action at all. Without this, even the most measured among us may find ourselves making decisions based on faulty premises and emotional reactions.

It is important to recognise that circumstance and luck play their part in every victory, this is a fact forgotten only by the foolish and those seeking undeserved glory and bragging rights. Those who achieve success yet fail to humble themselves by publicly recognising that a large part of their success is due to luck and the support of others will inevitably stir up envy in those around them, who will then work behind the scenes to undermine and devalue any achievements made. Be wary of the envious, you will not see them coming and they will never forgive you for your success.

Afterword

During the planning process for the **Secrets of The Dark Arts** series, it was clear that the primary aim of the collection should be to empower the individual and provide the communication and interpersonal skill required to break new ground and achieve success in both personal development and relationships. All interactions contain some form of persuasion, influence or outright manipulation and through reading this book you have learned how to recognise and direct such interactions towards your own goals. The methods described were chosen for their passive nature and flexibility. The more flexible and patient your style, the more credible and influential you will ultimately become. To accomplish this, you must adopt a style of formlessness, impossible to grasp or fathom, and therefore impossible to attack. Planning multiple steps ahead and playing the long game wherever possible is the essence of this formless, fluid style. When your current actions are related to events in the future, they cannot be comprehended by those who 'think' in the present and even individuals with foresight and experience will be unable to define your overall goal. Your intentions are elusive and cannot be figured out. With nothing to grasp, others will become bored of trying to understand your underlying motives and therefore they will be largely ignored as people focus only on current issues, they can sink their teeth into, most people are interested in complaining or good old gossip and so if you give them nothing to chew on they will move on. By practicing the skills in this book, you will, without a doubt improve upon your current skillset and move closer towards achieving your lifetime goals, I wish you the best of luck.

If you wish to learn more about covert persuasion, influence, and analyzing others look to the first book in the **Secrets of The Dark Arts** series **Psychological Manipulation: Analyzing People, Situations and How to Influence Others Through Covert Persuasion.**

Notes

Notes

Notes

Notes

Notes